PETER MAYLE

PROVENCE

PROVENCE

PETER MAYLE

Aerial Photography by

JASON HAWKES

RANDOM HOUSE

TEXT © Peter Mayle 1994
PHOTOGRAPHY © Aerial Images Ltd 1994

All rights reserved under International and
Pan-American Copyright Conventions.
Published in the United States by Random House, Inc., New York,
and simultaneously in Canada by Random House of Canada Limited, Toronto.
Published in the United Kingdom by Weidenfeld & Nicolson.

Library of Congress Cataloging-in-Publication Data
Mayle, Peter.
    Provence / Peter Mayle: aerial photography by Jason Hawkes.
        p.   cm.
    ISBN 0-679-43564-6
    1. Provence (France) – Description and travel. 2. Provence
    (France) – Aerial photographs. I. Hawkes, Jason. II. Title.
    D0611.P968M383 1994
    944'.9'00222–dc20 94-16914

Canadian Cataloging in Publication Data
Mayle, Peter
    Provence

    ISBN 0-394-22433-7
    1. Provence (France) – Description and travel.
    2. Provence (France) – Pictorial works.
    I. Hawkes, Jason. II. Title

    DC611.P958M38 1994 914.4'904 C94-931442-0

DESIGNED BY The Bridgewater Book Company Limited

PHOTOGRAPHER'S ACKNOWLEDGEMENTS
We would like to thank Peter and Jennie Mayle
for their enthusiasm towards our idea for the book.
Our thanks also to all the ATCs and CPL(H)s
in southern France who helped us.

The photographs in this book may be obtained
from the Weidenfeld & Nicolson Photographic Archives,
telephone (0)71 498 3011 or fax (0)71 498 0748.
Many other photographs taken from the air
by Jason Hawkes are available from
the Jason Hawkes Aerial Collection, telephone (0)71 486 2800.

ENDPAPERS: *Villeneuve-lès-Avignon*

PAGE 1: *Yacht off les Calanques near Cassis*

PAGES 2-3: *Ménerbes*

CONTENTS

VOYAGE IN A BUBBLE

I BEGAN TO HAVE SECOND THOUGHTS about the whole idea when Jason Hawkes very kindly offered to lend me his thermal flying trousers. 'You'll need these,' he said. 'We've taken the side window off, and it gets a bit chilly.' I asked whether this technical adjustment was absolutely necessary. 'Oh yes,' he said, 'it means you can lean out and get a better view.'

Passengers waiting for the morning flight to Paris watched with interest as I wrestled with the trousers in a corner of the small departure lounge at Avignon airport – fast, sideways glances before they resumed their study of the Figaro. How were they to know that instead of joining them in a plane with a full complement of windows I was about to make my maiden voyage in a vest-pocket helicopter with a gaping hole in it?

On legs that had become suddenly fat in their thermal cocoons, I waddled out to the take-off area, where the pilot, Tim Kendall, was topping up with fuel. The helicopter, which looked quite small from a distance, seemed to diminish in size as I got closer, shrinking to the dimensions of a goldfish bowl built for two, open to the elements on the passenger side, tiny, shiny and, to my novice's eye, perilously fragile. Tim had flown it over from England, a seven-hour trip he claimed had been fun.

You don't get in to a machine of this kind; you insert yourself. And, if you've got any sense, you make sure that you keep your knees away from the joystick and your feet off the rudder bar. I had visions of an involuntary twitch of the leg sending us into a terminal spin and a nose-dive into the vines somewhere between Avignon and Ménerbes. Tim, who had obviously noticed the exaggerated delicacy with which I was arranging myself, told me to relax. I tried. I looked at the tarmac four feet below and fought back the first stirrings of vertigo.

LEFT: Local weather experts claim that Provence has 300 days of sunshine every year, and this is one of them. Light spills over the Lubéron, the plain turns gold and there's a smile on every hotel owner's face.

The fuselage of the helicopter ended just below my left knee. The bubble of the cockpit ended a few inches above my head. In between were wide open spaces. Captain Kendall told me to make sure my seat belt was securely fastened. It was an unnecessary instruction. If I'd had the wretched thing any tighter it would have broken a couple of ribs.

We took off, and it was the first of many pleasant surprises. Instead of the judder and rivet-popping effort of a normal aircraft take-off, there was nothing more than an increase in the level of engine noise and a

ABOVE: Ménerbes sits on its hill and takes in the sun. There are evenings when the village is so quiet you can hear the distant creak of shutters being opened two streets away.

ABOVE: *Clouds in the valley, looking thick enough to walk on. Walking through them as you climb the Lubéron is eerie but refreshing, and you arrive at the top damp.*

gentle, almost imperceptible, levitation. When I opened one fearful eye, Avignon airport was an orderly collection of toy buildings five hundred feet below. We turned east into the morning sun, and headed for the Lubéron. With the intercom earphones on, the engine was barely audible, and there was no sense of movement at all through the air. Below, on the main road into Avignon, cars moved silently, looking like brightly coloured minnows on the surface of a black stream. We floated above them, as calm as a stalled cloud. It was difficult to believe that we were travelling across the sky at a hundred miles an hour. I put one tentative hand out; the wind was a solid slab of cold air against my palm. Tim's voice came through the intercom. 'We're turning. Hold on.' The helicopter tilted, the angle of the horizon changed abruptly, and I had a strong desire to clutch at something substantial, even the pilot's leg. A few millimetres of webbing, at moments like this, are not quite enough to overcome the realization that you are suspended in an unnatural fashion, without any layers of Plexiglas and fuselage between you and a long and picturesque drop. I was delighted when the horizon resumed its proper, level place.

We passed over Cavaillon and began to follow the line of the road I have taken hundreds of times by car, the road home. Coming in low over Ménerbes, I could see a knot of people outside the post office. Not a single head looked up. Helicopters are not uncommon in the valley. The story is that they are used by officials who concern themselves with such matters to make sure that nobody is committing the grave offence against the state of building an illicit swimming pool. For this, one needs a permit. Woe betide the lawbreaker who tries to hide his pool behind trees and hedges. The *piscine* patrol will find him, and retribution will follow.

We lost altitude as we approached our house, and hovered over the deep gash made in the vineyard by one of the spring storms, when several inches of rain had fallen in the space of two or three hours. We had been lucky, with nothing to show for the deluge but a slanting trench four feet deep that sliced through the vines. Less fortunate people, like the inhabitants of Vaison-la-Romaine, had lost cars and even houses. It was hard to imagine such destructive violence on a calm, sunny morning.

Even lower now, we flew over to the house, and the helicopter's shadow settled on the roof. My wife came out and waved, the dogs capered in the courtyard, and I noticed that the pool needed cleaning. In times of forest fires, the *pompiers* are said to use specially equipped helicopters – flying suction pumps – that can drain the water from your pool to drop on the flames. This had always struck me as another highly improbable Provençal tale. But now, from my motionless vantage point fifty feet above the shallow end, it seemed quite possible. As Tim had told me, helicopters can do practically anything except mow the lawn.

RIGHT: *St-Rémy is one of the more fashionable towns in Provence, and – surrounded by plane trees, overlooked by the Alpilles – one of the most attractive. Good cafés, too.*

We turned and rose, and climbed to the top of the mountains behind the house – one minute, compared with nearly an hour of hard slog on foot. The view unrolled to the south, ending with the distant glint of the Mediterranean. To the north, the valley floors were still under thick carpets of morning mist, pierced by treetops and the lumpy grey snouts of crags. A pair of magpies, crisp in their black and white plumage, left their private tree and flew off, probably complaining about the noise. It was odd to be looking at birds from above.

Following the line of the forest road than runs along the crest of the Lubéron, we paused over the quarry at Ménerbes, where years of gnawing by mechanical teeth have transformed the lower slope of the mountain into an amphitheatre, walled by stark, straight-edged scars. This gradual nibbling of the mountain, unsightly though it is, provides a wonderfully creamy stone that a skilled artisan can carve like soap. Corners are rounded, edges are rolled, the appearance of hardness disappears, and you are somehow surprised that it doesn't dent under the pressure of a prodding finger.

BELOW: *The Palais des Papes, with its gardens above the Rhône and the Pont d'Avignon arching across the river. Dancers should proceed with caution: the bridge stops short before reaching the other side.*

Eight hundred years before the invention of helicopters, the village of Oppède, now called Oppède-le-Vieux, grew up around the castle that first belonged to the Counts of Forcalquier. Over the centuries, the castle changed hands and the villagers emigrated downhill to easier, less precipitous land. They left behind them, at the very top of the old village, the little church of Notre-Dame-d'Alydon. Looking down on it from the comfort of my aerial armchair, I tried to imagine the extraordinary effort that must have gone into building it on a solitary rock surrounded by land that, from above, appeared to fall away as steeply as a cliff. No bulldozers, no hydraulic cranes, no electricity, every stone brought uphill by man or donkey, cut and smoothed and placed by hand. But why there? Why not on flatter land at the bottom of the village? And then I remembered what an old man had once told me when I was looking around a tiny village cemetery set in the most spectacular position. God gets the best views, he had said. Obviously, the same rule applied in the twelfth century.

The contrast between the church on the mountain side and the sprawl of Cavaillon, with its perpetual procession of long-distance trucks, was startling, as if we had flown through hundreds of years in a matter of minutes. We crossed the meagre, mud-coloured flow of the Durance river, and the autoroute that half of Europe takes each summer to go down to the Côte d'Azur, and headed across the plain towards Saint-Rémy and its miniature mountain range.

By now, I was starting to feel less like a petrified diver on a thirty-foot board and more comfortable. Encouraged by the confident nonchalance with which Captain Kendall was dealing with the controls, I thought I'd lean out for a breath of air, and caught a whiff of woodsmoke from a bonfire far below. You can't do that in 747, nor do you ever have the strange and wonderful sensation of flying through your own rainbow.

Apparently, it's quite normal. Tim changed course and headed into the middle of a small cloud. On either side of us was what you'd expect – billows of regulation, grey-white mist. But immediately ahead was a pale, multi-coloured curtain, dancing in the light as delicate as gauze. There is a scientific explanation for this, which has to do with engine emissions and rotor blade action. There is even, I suspect, a mathematical formula for it. But for me it was a moment of magic, unexpected and physically thrilling.

We came back into the blue, and I could see the jagged, bone-white limestone fangs of Les Alpilles rising up from the level land to the west of Saint-Rémy. As mountain ranges go, it is a mere baby, decorative from a distance, almost cosy. This changes abruptly on closer inspection. Once amongst the peaks and crags the harshness becomes more apparent, and as we flew through them I felt that we might easily be exploring some sinister corner of the moon rather than one of the most fashionable parts of Provence.

ABOVE AND OVERLEAF: *No kinks, no curves, no deviations from the straight and narrow – it is almost as if the tractor has been going up and down on rails.*

Fashion made a reappearance in the form of a neat little golf course and the village of Les Baux, once famous for bauxite and now better known for tourism and gastronomy. The pool and terrace restaurant of the Baumanière slipped below us, and I was tempted to ask Tim if he could squeeze us in next to the Mercedes and the BMWs in the hotel car park. Flying, I discovered, gives me a voracious appetite. It probably has something to do with the after-effects of fear.

Le Pont *célèbre* came into view – the subject of a song, thousands of postcards and tens of thousands of holiday snaps. In fact, it is less than half a bridge, reduced from its original twenty-two arches to four, because the good people of Avignon found the cost of upkeep and repair too much for them. Did they dance on it before it crumbled away? Probably not, say the historians. They danced underneath it, on the Ile de la Barthelasse in the middle of the river.

From Avignon to anti-climax. Back on the ground, stripped of the thermal trousers, and having to dodge the lethal swoops of the French motorist on his way to an early lunch, I found myself missing the peace and the exhilarating sensation of complete freedom that were the strongest impressions of my first helicopter flight.

And then, of course, there were the views, the three-dimensional map that gives you such a vivid sense of the countryside and how man has altered it, fought with it, neglected it, polluted it or even left it alone during the period of his extended tenancy.

There is evidence, mile upon meticulous mile of it, that a giant gardener has been at work with a green thumb and a long ruler. Straight lines are everywhere, forming precise, sharp patterns across the fields and on the hillsides. You see, on adjoining pieces of land, that one block of vines has been planted north to south, while their next door neighbour's march from east to west, and you can be sure that this has been a matter of considerable thought and debate. Monsieur Dupont (north to south) will undoubtedly take the view that he has gauged the lie of the land and the angle of the sun correctly. The disposition of his vines is perfectly suited to the *micro-climat*, and will therefore produce a grape of formidable succulence. Monsieur Fernand (east to west) will have a similarly firm opinion of the placement of his own vines. They will nod amiably as their tractors pass while allowing themselves a secret moment of satisfaction, and perhaps a quiet sigh of sympathy, at the misguided decision of the other.

The slim ranks of vines are broken up, from time to time, by larger clumps, equally carefully arranged, of cherry trees. In the summer, they resemble wilted green umbrellas. In the winter, bundles of twigs splashed with turquoise, almost luminous splashes of pesticide. And there is one moment, usually in May, when they put on a show that rivals any firework display. Blossom, starting as small explosions scattered through the trees, turns into an uninterrupted pink and white sea which lasts, if there isn't any wind, for perhaps two weeks. Blossom is followed by fruit, and fruit is followed by the cherry-pickers on their triangular wooden ladders. The ladders, of course, are invisible from above. All you see, rather disconcertingly, are treetops that suddenly sprout a brown arm or a cloth cap as the picker stretches for a high bunch.

ABOVE: *A field in the Camargue, looking more like a piece of modern art or a large-scale exercise in geometry than a watering system.*

The only crop in the valley that defies the rules of geometric discipline is the melon. Clusters of them sprawl across the fields in nests, almost always, in the season, under the surveillance of a stooped, slow-moving figure. He will be judging ripeness, culling the melons that he considers ready for the short trip to the market in Cavaillon or the longer, more lucrative voyage to Paris. His natural enemies, as the summer heat rises and water levels drop, are the wild boar that live in the mountains. At the end of a dry day, they will come down looking for moisture, trampling gardens, invading swimming pools, rooting among flower-beds, and crossing roads with a grand disdain for Renaults and Citroens. To a thirsty boar, the promise of a melon in the cool of the evening is irresistible. But not any old melon. He has a

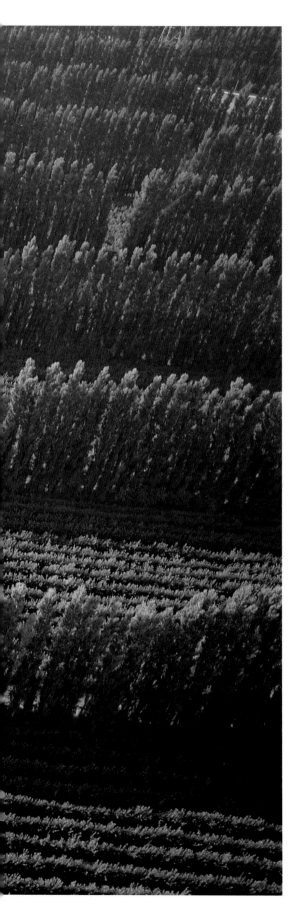

connoisseur's discrimination. Only the ripe ones – the ones that were going to market the next morning – are good enough. To make the farmer's life even more frustrating, the ripening season for melons does not coincide with the hunting season for boar. The gun must stay in its cupboard, while the trespasser eats his fill and reflects on the generosity of nature. It's enough to make a man turn his back on the melon and take up mushroom-growing.

Or, if he's prepared to move out of the valley and up into the hills, he could try his hand at the most spectacular crop of all: lavender.

Even on the bleakest January day, a lavender field is a satisfying sight. Cropped into rounded, spiky tussocks, the bushes form continuous, undulating lines, as though a colony of hedgehogs were hibernating, nose to tail, across the countryside. The grey stubble of winter becomes green shoots in spring, and then, one day in summer, the entire field takes on a purple blur – a purple which deepens and strengthens before reaching its peak, some time in July, in a dense swathe of colour that almost makes your eyes ache.

That is enough of a reward in itself for the man lucky enough to have a lavender patch, but it doesn't end there. Lavender is fodder for bees, and if you put hives by the side of your field, you will have scented honey for breakfast. Lavender essence perfumes your soap and your bath. Lavender lotion soothes the skin that has been bitten by insects or reddened by the sun. Dried lavender makes wardrobes and drawers a pleasure to open, and last summer's lavender tossed onto the first fire of winter fills the house with the fragrance of July. They even say that gargling with a lavender *tisane* will cleanse and purify the system and stimulate internal *joie de vivre*. And on a practical note which will be appreciated by any Provençal farmer, lavender plays no part in a wild boar's diet.

Not all the efforts of centuries of cultivation have been directed at crops, and from the air you can see some wonderfully graphic examples of defensive gardening. Trees have been used for protection – against the battering of the Mistral, and the hammer of the sun.

LEFT: *Poplars on parade, catching the last slants of sun near Le Thor, outside Avignon. A particularly tasty mushroom sometimes grows at the base of these trees, as big as a beret and as juicy as steak.*

RIGHT: *A sandwich of plane trees, part of the Cours Mirabeau in Aix-en-Provence, the street where Cézanne grew up.*

Horror stories about the Mistral – that it causes ennui or madness, that it skims precious layers of topsoil from the land, that it turns the milk sour in nursing goats, even that it blows lightweight human beings off cliffs – are told with great relish and considerable embroidery. Nevertheless, it is a malevolent wind, nagging and enervating in summer, biting and viciously cold in winter. In your car, you can watch the wind thrashing through the landscape from the privileged position of an insulated observer, and marvel at its force. But if your work is in the fields, that force is aimed at you – stinging your eyes, whipping your skin, applying a freezing compress to your back, plucking your hat from your head and making you long for a snug job in the village post office. And so, over the years, farmers have fought back. Knowing that the Mistral invariably attacks from the west, they have put up barricades of cypress trees, planted so tightly that nothing wider than an emaciated dog could pass between the trunks. You will see windbreaks like this hundreds of yards long, slanted across the plains at an angle precisely calculated to block – or at least dilute – the torrent of air that has funnelled its way down the Rhône valley and has come looking for your kidneys.

Another of nature's favourite targets is the top of your skull, and anyone who has stood for a moment too long in the oven of midday during July or August will remember the experience. A magnifying glass seems to have been positioned directly above your head. Your hair turns warm. Your scalp perspires. You look for shade, and more often than not you find it, along the roadside, in village squares or town boulevards, beneath the thick leafy canopy of a plane tree.

In other parts of the world, the plane tree is permitted to grow upwards, like any other normal tree whose ambitions are vertical rather than horizontal. But not in Provence. Here, the plane tree is regarded, from birth, as a potential parasol, and trained accordingly. The first falling of leaves in the autumn is the signal for swarms of pruners to appear. With a strictness that verges on brutality, they clip and saw and slice until all that remains is a trunk topped by gnarled, arthritic knuckles. It seems impossible for any living thing to flourish after such severe surgery, and yet, each spring, the knuckles push out optimistic sprigs, more sideways than upwards if the pruning has been correctly carried out, and by summer – *voilà*! One has shade.

There are two particularly beautiful and impressive stretches of plane trees, not far from where we live, and they always make me admire the foresight of the men who planted them in the eighteenth century. The first is the avenue several kilometres long – and, of course, dead straight – that leads into Saint-Rémy from the east. Driving down this road in the summer, you travel in a continuous, hypnotic strobe of light and shadow. Flying above it, you can see cars flicker and vanish and reappear.

The second display, not as long, but equally straight and much better known, is the ornamental five hundred yards of the Cours Mirabeau, Cézanne's old address in Aix-en-Provence. The Cours has been called `the most satisfying street in France', and while the architectural proportions are ideal and the fountains decorative and cooling, for me the street is made by its two high and handsome lines of plane trees. Every time I go to Aix, I take my hat off to the master gardener responsible, knowing that, thanks to him, my bare head is safe from the sun. And I often wonder what his predecessors, the founders of Aix, would think if they could see how the old place has grown.

It was the first Roman settlement in Gaul, founded in 123 BC and called Aquae Sextiae because of the thermal springs (one of them, the Fontaine d'Eau Chaude, is still trickling its 34-degree water in the Cours Mirabeau). In those days, the Romans kept themselves astonishingly busy. After a hectic time fighting Salians, Teutons and any other interlopers foolish enough to try their chances, you might think that there would be little energy left over, but not a bit of it. Vine-planting, road construction, town planning, bridge-building and, for a little light relief, the erection of classical monuments and triumphal arches, was all part of the day's work too. All over Provence, you can see traces – and sometimes much more than traces – of the Roman occupation.

From the air, you obviously miss the niceties of monuments and sculpture, but in compensation you are given views no Romans ever had of their achievements so many years ago. There are dozens, but from them all I would pick the theatre at Orange, south of Vaison-la-Romaine. Orange is now a town with about 30,000 inhabitants, but in Roman days nearly three times as many people lived there, and the theatre could hold ten thousand of them at a time. It is in the form of a massive D (the straight wall that joins the ends of the semi-circle is more than 300 feet long), and the curved banks of stone seats have

BELOW: *The Pont du Gard, which impressed Tobias Smollett (not a man given to extravagant praise) to such an extent that he compared it to Westminster Bridge. It is unlikely that the Romans who built it would have been flattered.*

ABOVE: *Gordes posing in the sunset, looking like a village specially constructed for the benefit of photographers, complete with cobbled streets and a Renaissance castle.*

ABOVE: *Mountains east of Vaison-la-Romaine, a haven for lovers of solitude. You won't bump into many people between here and Italy.*

been made by scooping out half a hillside. It is theatrical engineering of a weight and scale that would have made Shakespeare want to give up the Globe and emigrate.

Considering the thousands of years that Provence has been inhabited, cultivated and invaded, from Greeks and Romans to the hordes that now come down the autoroute from the north, it is remarkably empty. You will find this difficult to believe if you have ever spent two weeks disputing possession of a six-foot patch of beach on the Côte d'Azur with a boisterous family from Munich, or if you try to find a parking spot during the festival in Avignon, but it's true. And from the air, it's very apparent.

From Gordes – the centre of an area that is blessed, so they say, with the highest concentration of swimming pools in Europe, and more than its fair share of cars – a ten-minute flight to the north-west will take you to the middle of nowhere. You are over wilderness. If you see flocks of sheep, you're probably not far from Sisteron, whose herb-scented lamb is one of the great treats of Provence. Otherwise, signs of life are rare. The occasional car corkscrews through the mountain roads, and you may find yourself sharing air space with a startled buzzard, but the Alpes de Haute Provence are uncongested, unspoilt, wild and still. They used to be called the Basses Alpes, but the official bureau in charge of labelling parts of France must have thought that 'Low Alps' sounded too insignificant, and so, for the greater glory of the French *patrimoine*, the name was changed in a way that avoided having to go into details of alp height.

Flying over some parts of Haute Provence, you can sometimes feel that it's June down below, even though the calendar says February. The sun is still bright, although lower, and the rock and scrub and tough little evergreen oaks look no different at zero degrees than in midsummer. But further south, back towards the coast where the land is richer and flatter, there's no mistaking the time of year. The change of the seasons, often spectacular at ground level, is breathtaking from the air.

You enjoy the grand perspective. Instead of the normal, relatively close-up view of leaves and trees, you see entire forests change colour and texture. A single vineyard, fine sight though it is as it fades from green to yellow and rust in the autumn, is a daub compared to the full canvas of hundreds of acres and thousands of vines. Fields of sunflowers and stripes of lavender look as though they have been painted on the earth. The ripple of light and breeze turns olive groves from green to silver-grey and back to green again. Every prospect pleases.

For a time at least. And then you come to some of man's less attractive additions to the countryside – the concrete boxes have grown up around medieval villages, the miles of plastic greenhouses, the refinery on the coast at Berre with its permanent belch of fumes, the electricity pylons that have been unerringly placed on the crests of hills for maximum visibility. They're necessary, of course, all of them. But why do they have to be so ugly? I couldn't help wishing that the Romans were still in charge of public works.

But blots on the landscape are relatively rare, and nowhere rarer than around the various enclaves that have been settled by the celebrities of the day – politicians, movie stars, tycoons and other eminent figures in search of sun and peace and privacy. This, inevitably, has attracted the keen interest of any journalist with a head for heights, and has led to the emergence of another regular summer visitor, the flying Peeping Tom.

All it takes to set him off is the whisper of a rumour, overheard in a village café or a chic little restaurant, that a well-known name has bought a house in Provence. If subsequent investigation shows this to be true, the property will first be scouted at ground level to check ease of access, availability of bushes to hide behind and the opportunities that exist for the creative use of a long-lens camera. More often that not, because the owner clearly doesn't want to be disturbed, the property has been chosen because of its well-hidden position, its long driveway secured by gates, its lack of neighbours and its invisibility to the casual passer-by. It is, so the owner fondly believes, completely protected from the outside world, a haven of rest to escape to after the rigours of public life.

And so it would have been, except for the helicopter.

For several years now, the helicopter has been used as an

BELOW: *A field of sunflowers in Van Gogh country near St-Rémy, where he spent his sad, mad last year in the asylum.*

RIGHT: *Anyone wanting*
to swim here, just along the
coast from Cassis, will have to
come by boat or on foot.
But the water's worth it —
clean, clear and uncrowded.

aerial foot in the door, uninvited and unwanted, swooping low in the hope of catching a distinguished sunbather *tout nu*. French magazines, in those long summer months when there is apparently no news, regularly devote dozens of full-colour pages to the roofs and swimming pools of the famous. As we look at one similar view after another, we are told how fascinating they are.

Here, for instance, we see Princess Caroline of Monaco's rosemary hedge. There is Jack Lang's barbecue area, or Gérard Depardieu's *boules* court, or the terrace on which President Mittérand is reputed to have once had lunch, or – yes, there it is in the corner – the van belonging to Terence Conran's gardener. Occasionally, we are rewarded with the sight of a genuine, albeit foreshortened, human figure, squinting angrily up into the sun. Who is it? Who cares? And yet, as sure as an August traffic jam in Saint-Tropez, we know that it will happen again this summer. Peeping Tom will fly once more to give us another series of roof tiles masquerading as exclusive revelations.

Nature's address book is altogether more interesting, partly because of the remarkable changes in atmosphere and character that can take place in the course of a single day. A village that looks cheerful at dawn and welcoming at noon becomes grim and faintly sinister as the light slips away to the west. The shadows settle and thicken, the streets empty, the shutters close and cats that have dozed all day in the sun begin to hurry home, always close to the walls, as though they're late. And, off in the distance, rising above everything, is the darkening bulk of the geological curiosity that is called, with uncomfortable accuracy, the windy mountain.

Mont Ventoux is the highest mountain in France between the Alps and the Pyrenees, and there's no chance of mistaking it. Ventoux is bald, and its summit is permanently, sometimes blindingly, white – not, for most of the year, with snow, but with rocks and fragments of limestone. The impression you have, when standing on the crest, is that a construction gang has started work and then given up, leaving the job unfinished. And one could hardly blame them. On a day when the wind is burrowing through your clothes and into your bones, it is a hard, raw place, a place you leave with a shudder before going back down into a Mediterranean climate. Like a violent thunderstorm, Mont Ventoux is best appreciated from a distance. And yet, for hundreds of years, the challenge of getting to the top has caused men to endure discomfort, exhaustion, dehydration or worse.

The first recorded climb was made in 1327 by the poet Petrarch. It took him an entire day of effort, and it led him to write a detailed description – not in poetry, but in Latin – of the mountain's odd characteristics, from its gravel cap to the perfect conical shadow it casts at sunrise and sunset.

Centuries later, the British racing cyclist Tommy Simpson died while making the climb. They say it was a heart attack, and they built a small monument to mark the spot – and perhaps to warn other athletes that there is a limit to what the human body can do. I was half-expecting disaster last year, when my son insisted that he could run to the top. He did, just, but he was unnaturally quiet for a day or two afterwards. I don't think he'll try it again. His experience, which sounded deeply unpleasant, did much to reinforce my appreciation of the merits of ascent by helicopter.

In fact, it is sightseeing de luxe. The cars that clot summer roads and make driving an overheated, ill-tempered obstacle course are left to growl at each other far below. You are free, and in a single morning you can see the seaside vineyards of Cassis, the red rocks of the Esterel, the lagoons and flamingoes of the Camargue, the Renaissance castle of Lourmarin, the ruins of the Marquis de Sade's château at Lacoste – the world is yours, and if you want to pause and look more closely, you can.

You see earlier, and bigger, sunrises than people who are anchored to the ground can see, and later, more lingering sunsets, when your neighbours are often those long, cigar-shaped clouds, tinged to an improbable pink, that decorate the evenings in Provence. You float, and wonder how Cézanne or Van Gogh would have felt to see their landscapes from a perch in the sky.

But those are the luxuries of the amateur spectator, the passenger with nothing to do except enjoy this minuscule room with a view. It's very different for the workers.

The qualifications for the job are demanding and occasionally terrifying. Both photographer and pilot must be prepared to get up well before dawn, a time when most of us feel far from our best, so that they can catch the morning as it arrives. Often, because of too much mist or turbulence, it's not worth going up. The middle of the day, when the mist has gone and perhaps the wind has dropped, is no good; the sun is too high and the light is too flat. Nothing can be done except to spend a frustrating day waiting for evening.

BELOW: *Penthouses overlooking Nice.*
On a clear day you can look across
the Baie des Anges and do some yacht-spotting
as millionaire sailors drift in and out of the port.

RIGHT: Sur la plage *at Cassis. Further along the coast, the view would be very different, and you wouldn't be able to see the sand for people.*

If the weather is kind and the light is falling the way it should, you may think that the photographer's task is simple: get the right exposure, point and shoot. And it is simple. You or I could do it, and we would produce hundreds of truly banal photographs. But to create an image that surprises, you need the ability to see differently, whether your subject is beautiful, mundane or even ugly. You need the eye.

With the eye, an unprepossessing heap of rotting tomatoes becomes a lurid, almost surreal mountain range; a railway shunting yard takes on the appearance of a handless clock; shadows on the ground seem to have the substance of buildings; villages look like giant boats of stone moored among the vines. And imagine what it took to get the picture.

You are travelling at a hundred miles an hour when your eye is taken by a particular arrangement of light and landscape. You slow down, you hover, you tilt. Defying every instinct, you hang yourself out of the cockpit, the top half of your body fully exposed to the suck of gravity – and then you're supposed to disregard these unconventional conditions while you attend to the fine points of focus and exposure. It is, to me, an astonishing act of faith, not only total trust in those few millimetres of webbing across your chest, but also in your pilot.

I was once allowed, for a few closely supervised seconds, to take over as novice pilot. It was a still, windless day. Up until the takeover, it had been a completely smooth flight. And it all looked so easy.

It isn't. The controls respond to a tremor from your fingers. If you shift fractionally in your seat, your foot exerts a twitch of pressure on a rudder bar, and the obedient helicopter does something instant, unplanned and disconcerting. It was a lesson to me in the careless way in which we normally move, and I was suddenly aware of the steadiness and skill required to fly through the air and make nothing happen.

The combination of Hawkes and Kendall, the eye and the hand, has shown me how much I didn't know about Provence, and how much I haven't seen. I can hardly wait to put on the thermal trousers again.

ABOVE: *The end of another sunny day in Marseille,*
and you can be sure that the pastis bottles are coming out
all over the city.

NORTH

From Mont Ventoux to Avignon
and the Grand Canyon du Verdon

East of Vaison-la-Romaine and north of the more densely populated Vaucluse, the region changes its name and becomes empty. The Alpes de Haute Provence stretch away to the end of France, sometimes green, sometimes blue, sometimes grey. There are inhabitants — some of the tastiest and, for that reason, the most famous sheep in the country — and there are a few roads. But it is not a place for the gregarious holidaymaker, or anyone who feels uncomfortable out of sight of buildings. Below Barcelonette, the most northerly town in Provence, you will find the national park of Mercantour, a hiker's paradise, and the home of eagles, falcons, chamois, ibex and wild boar. With stout heart and boots, you can walk from here into Italy.

The village and perched church of Mollans-sur-Ouvèze. No self-respecting village in Provence is without at least one church, and many of them are fascinating, either as architectural feats or because they contain an obscure but highly prized relic. The difficulty often comes when you try to get in to see it. Some churches are closed all day, except for Mass. Some are open all day, except for lunch. If the church door resists your push, the best thing to do is go to the Mairie (but again, not at lunchtime) or to the local priest's house, the presbytère, *and ask to borrow the key.*

Vaison-la-Romaine was once (nearly two thousand years ago) a town of such notable affluence that it was described, with a touch of Latin hyperbole, as urbs opulentissima. And, naturally, no urbs as opulent as Vaison could be without its own theatre, part of which you see here. Like the theatre in Orange, it is still used today during the summer festival of music and drama. Signs of Roman times are everywhere in Vaison, on the streets or in the museum, and it is a place of endless interest to anyone with any eye for history. Or, indeed, for anyone with a taste for wine. Vaison is on the edge of Côtes-du-Rhône country, and in the Maison du Vin you can spend an instructive and increasingly happy afternoon doing your research into the best of the local wines.

The village of St-Étienne-des-Sorts casts its shadow – which resembles one of Walt Disney's skylines – on the waters of the Rhône. Since the arrival of trains and planes and autoroutes, the river is not the trade highway it used to be, but is still, if you believe some of the legends, the home of a man-eating monster called the Tarasque. A very old man once told me that the aunt of a distant cousin of his great-grandfather had witnessed the snatching of a maiden from the river bank. Three glasses of pastis later, the maiden had expanded into a group of virgins. Alas, there is very little scientific evidence to confirm this tragic tale.

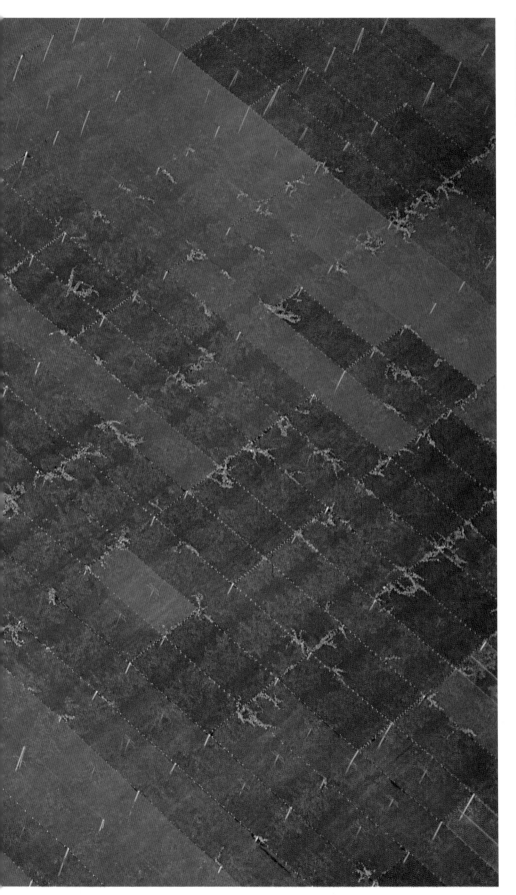

Agricultural symmetry in the countryside round Orange. I often wonder how the Provençal farmer – addicted as he is to precisely spaced regimentation – would cope with anything as untidy as livestock. A herd of cows, for instance, with their infuriating tendency to either group or straggle, would drive him mad. Although, knowing him, he'd probably train them to graze in lines of three abreast so that they wouldn't offend his sense of order.

The theatre at Orange, with the wall that Louis XIV complimented in a quotation that has survived the centuries: 'The best wall in my kingdom', he is supposed to have said, and it is a sight to impress the most jaded wall connoisseur - 335 feet long, 120 feet high, and still in remarkably good condition nearly two thousand years after the Romans built it. A fine statue of Caesar Augustus looks out over the seats which, on a good night, can be buzzing with ten thousand people.

Unsheathe your corkscrew. This is Châteauneuf-du-Pape, where some of the best and strongest wines in Provence are made, and where the modern system of appellation contrôlée was born in the early 1920s. The growers here are serious men, constantly on the lookout to ward off threats to their immaculate and highly profitable vines. Forty years ago, when newspapers reported sightings of flying saucers (locally known as 'cigares volants'), the elders of the village leapt into action, passing a decree that flying cigars were absolutely forbidden to land anywhere in the commune. It worked.

LEFT

The town of Carpentras, once ruled by the Pope and run by bishops, is the capital of the département of the Vaucluse and the centre of the Provençal truffle trade. From December until February, the Friday morning market is a study in the techniques of sniffing, weighing and haggling as prices are fixed and cash (never a cheque) changes hands. The other gastronomic speciality of Carpentras is a mint-flavoured sweet called a berlingot. Sucking one helps to concentrate the mind as you try to negotiate the town's one-way ring of boulevards that local admirers of Alain Prost use for speed trials.

ABOVE

Turrets and crenellations at Montfaucon, near Roquemaure. The architectural style is particularly well suited to the reclusive owner who wishes to avoid the attentions of the outside world. If unwelcome visitors persist, despite locked doors and shuttered windows, a well-aimed cauldron of boiling oil, poured from one of the turrets, will always do the trick. Which reminds me of a marvellously misanthropic warning notice I once saw at the edge of a private hunting reserve in the Var. Roughly translated, it read: 'Trespassers will be shot. Survivors will be prosecuted.'

LEFT

Venasque seems permanently poised to slide off its site and slip further down the Ventoux foothills. Seeing it now, small and somnolent, it is hard to believe that it was the capital of the Comtat-Venaissin, an area which roughly corresponded to the Vaucluse of today. There are ramparts, and a baptistery that dates from the sixth century, but very few other signs of ancient grandeur. The beautiful views are still there, though, and one modern consolation in the form of an excellent restaurant. La Fontaine. It's in the tiny square where, not surprisingly, you will find a fountain.

RIGHT

The traditional colours of Provence, reproduced on countless pennants and flags and car stickers and pastis labels, are yellow and red. The blue of the sky is an obvious addition. But what I still find surprising is the greenness. There is, of course, less of it in the winter, mainly scrub oak and cypress and rosemary, but when spring comes the countryside glows with every shade of green imaginable, from the brightness of new vine leaves to the more restrained foliage of almond and cherry and plane trees. And the fields, like these in the Vaucluse, have an almost English lushness about them.

39

R I G H T

Provençal roads vary wildly from the rigid straightness beloved by transport planners and drivers of supercharged Renault 5s to the meandering loops and hairpins of the back country. Sometimes the detours are caused by rock formations that are too big to blow up; sometimes, as you see here, they are to accommodate private land. If you continue along this road you'll find one of the most charming little towns in the Vaucluse, Pernes-les-Fontaines, with more fountains than most cities. I tried to count them, and gave up after 36. I was later told I missed one.

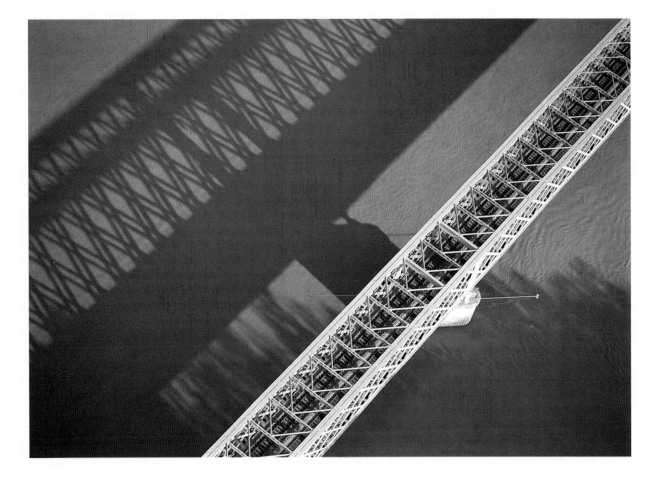

A railway bridge that spans the Rhône, north of Avignon. The high-speed service linking Provence to Paris, the TGV, does the trip in less than four hours – comfortable, clean and very seldom late. Inspired, no doubt, by their success in the south, the French railway authorities created the 'Ligne Napoléon' to take passengers from Paris through the Channel tunnel to England. It is said that, in a rare flash of bureaucratic humour, the French proposed that their Napoleon train should be permitted to arrive in London at Waterloo station. Descendants of the Duke of Wellington were not available for comment.

Villeneuve-lès-Avignon, the 'new town' on the old frontier between the kingdom of France and the Papal territories across the river. Now that there is little risk of invasion from Avignon, Villeneuve is a sleepy, pleasant place, and the home of some extraordinary works of art. There is an ivory statue of the Virgin Mary, carved in the fourteenth century, a double-faced Virgin, and Quarton's Coronation of the Virgin, a painting that includes not only saints and kings, heaven and hell, but one or two local landmarks as well. Pope Innocent VI was buried in Villeneuve. From Philippe-le-Bel's tower, originally built six hundred years ago to guard the approach to the bridge, you have fine views of Avignon and Mont Ventoux. And, at the end of a day of history, you can retire to the comfort of a converted sixteenth-century priory.

Avignon has received some unkind reviews over the years. Petrarch, for instance, was appalled: 'The hell of living people,' he called it, 'the thoroughfare of vice, the sewers of the earth.' Victor Hugo, possibly after noticing the excessive enthusiasm with which arguments were conducted, wrote: 'In Paris one quarrels, in Avignon one kills.' And the blood still runs hot. The spectacle of two Avignonnais locking horns over a disputed parking meter is high drama, filled with sound and arm-waving fury. It's a lively place.

It was perhaps even more lively, and certainly more dangerous, when it was the headquarters of Christianity during the fourteenth century. Clement V was the first Pope to turn his back on Rome in favour of Avignon, and Gregory XI was the last. In between were almost seventy years of prosperity and all that prosperity brings, from artists and master builders to prostitutes and street gangs. Dirt, disease, debauchery and violence were the order of the day – unless, of course, you were part of the protected papal entourage, in which case you sheltered behind massive stone walls in considerable luxury. The closest we come to those stirring times now is during the annual arts festival, when the streets teem with actors, clowns, musicians, mime artists, bemused tourists and irascible gendarmes, all of them watched over, I suspect, by the disapproving ghost of Petrarch.

The bridge. Its formal title is the Pont St-Bénézet, commemorating the shepherd boy Bénézet who, so legend tells us, laid the foundation stones in the twelfth century. It is open for dancing, or just as a vantage point. The view back towards Avignon is impressive rather than lyrical – the great wall of the Rocher des Doms and, behind it, the equally unwelcoming bulk of the Palais des Papes (not only a papal palace in its time, but also a barracks and a prison).

44

In grimy contrast to the sleek aerodynamic shape of the high–speed TGV, some more venerable
examples of French rolling stock gather here in a shunting yard at Avignon station. It may not
be pretty, but at least it's functional, unlike the vortex of madness at the front of the station.
This, for future reference, is an area to avoid. The designer in chief of car parks has done his
worst, creating an island of chaos for motorists anxious to catch their trains. For difficulty of
access, for ease of collision, for mounting panic and bad temper – few places on earth can have
been so cunningly created to cause the traveller to wish he had stayed at home.

The final resting place, outside Avignon, of a herd of dead trucks. In their younger days, they
would have hissed and rumbled their way across France, usually driven by large, meaty men. It
is not often you see a slender truck driver, possibly because of the relais routier – the network
of truckers' restaurants notable for their giant parking areas and excellent value for money.
After a simple but good three-course meal with wine, there will still be change from 100 francs,
and the routier will feel sufficiently refreshed to eat up another few hundred kilometres before
dark. (In pre-truck days, routiers were the villains of Avignon, private armies who would
come into town for some enthusiastic pillaging unless the Pope paid them to go away.)

Here you see a testament to an unknown tractor driver. Nothing mars the precious straightness - no zig-zags, no skid marks, no blemishes caused by a careless moment at the wheel, no crooked or even slightly deviant line and, heaven forbid, no loose and undisciplined wobbles. It looks easy, driving a tractor. Up one side, down the next, average speed three miles an hour. What could be more simple? And yet, when you try it, you find that what looked like a flat field has suddenly developed slopes and grooves and contusions. Rocks spring up to twist the wheels out of true. Monotony makes the guiding hand lax. That is why, when I see land like this, near Avignon, I salute the gentleman with the cloth cap and the leathery face who has managed to stick to his straight and very narrow path.

ABOVE

One of the features of rural France is the manner in which the farmer shows his disapproval of the way the world is going. He is never short of targets for his anger - some new and ridiculous piece of legislation from Brussels, the nefarious behaviour of Spanish and Italian farmers, a rise in the price of diesel, a drop in the price of grapes - there is always something to upset him, and he often takes his revenge in messy and spectacular fashion. He dumps. He dumps melons on the steps of the Mairie, he dumps potatoes on the autoroute, he dumps cherries in the village fountain or, as he has done here, he dumps tomatoes on the banks of the Durance.

ABOVE

A field under wraps on the flat and fertile land between Avignon and Cavaillon, where vineyards are outnumbered by orchards – row after row of Les Golden *or maybe even* Les Granny, *the raw material for Provençal apple tarts. These are, for some reason, at their most inviting on Sunday mornings, when you go to the bakery with nothing more in mind than a loaf of bread. But there in the window are the tarts: pastry-rimmed wheels of wafer-thin slices, glistening with an apricot glaze and begging to be taken home. Diets are postponed until Monday.*

LEFT

Early, in the Rhône valley, before the sun has burned off the morning mist. In the autumn, this landscape will often look as though it has been planted with a forest of thin grey trees as the smoke from bonfires rises from the fields – the traditional way to dispose of the season's vine clippings. Bonfire rules, in theory if not always in practice, are strict: no burning between mid-April and mid-October, and no burning if the Mistral is blowing. Despite these precautions, every year seems to bring its crop of forest fires, and the terrifying sight of flames travelling faster than a man can run. Most of these fires, sadly, are started on purpose.

51

RIGHT

Provence changes colour dramatically every day, which must make life impossible for the artist who tries to capture the essence of the place in a single painting. There are the postcard colours of high noon – strong, hot, uncomplicated, often glaring. And then there are the pastels of morning and evening, the pink and faded mauve of the sky, the cream and grey and pale gold of stone, the soft, fuzzy green of vines and, as you see here behind Caumont-sur-Durance (outside Avignon), pools of mist the colour of lavender fields.

ABOVE

The island town of Isle-sur-la-Sorgue, near Fontaine-de-Vaucluse, the
setting for one of the prettiest Sunday markets in Provence, and the
centre of the antique dealers' mafia. They have colonized the old station
and taken over a stretch of the main road into town, which has antique
shops every twenty yards. And on market day, the brocanteurs are out
in force with whatever they've managed to salvage from attics and barns
throughout the Vaucluse: old books, mirrors, glasses, farm implements,
antique guns, severely wounded furniture – everything you could
imagine except, alas, a bargain. Console yourself with the local trout,
which are excellent.

OVERLEAF

Fontaine-de-Vaucluse, one of the earliest tourist attractions in Provence.
Until 1353, Petrarch spent a great deal of time here, and his admirers
have been coming for hundred of years. This is also where the river
Sorgue makes its appearance from the mouth of a cave at the foot of a
cliff, and in the spring it is not a modest appearance. The water has been
measured (as all things in France are measured) gushing out at 200 cubic
metres per second. In summer, the gush becomes a trickle, and tourists
who have come hoping to see a Provençal Niagara Falls look puzzled
and disappointed.

Every Monday morning, the centre of Cavaillon becomes a market, cars
are banished and the traffic jam is pedestrian. It has always been a rich
little town, and still has the reputation (energetically denied by local

Motorists paying their dues on the Autoroute de Soleil, which takes
millions of holidaymakers, in varying states of impatience and
frustration, down to the Côte d'Azur each summer. August, when most

ABOVE

The spun gold of sunlit mist over the Lubéron. In 1977, much of the area was turned into a Parc Régional, partly to protect it from property developers' rash, that unsightly affliction which creeps across fields and hillsides in the form of villas, usually constructed from lurid pink concrete. Another benefit of park status is that it encourages wildlife. Ironically, the people who preach loudest about preserving the habitat of birds and wild animals are often the same people who go into the mountains each winter to shoot them. But, as anyone who has ever tried to keep a determined hunter off the property knows, la chasse *is a sacred right. Anything edible is at risk. (That's why there are so many magpies in the Lubéron. Despite their culinary ingenuity and daring, the French draw the line at eating birds which have such suspect feeding habits, and there is no recipe that I know for magpie, whether boiled, roasted or* en croûte.*)*

RIGHT

The skyscapes in the Lubéron, like the land below, change quite noticeably with the seasons. Summer has its classic fleecy clouds or the long 'flying cigars' so unpopular in Châteauneuf-du-Pape. In winter, the clouds take on an extra whiteness and density, and they become more tenacious. It takes more than an hour or two of sunshine to clear them away, and there are days when they are so low that you can walk through them on your way to the top of the mountains. But not even the most stubborn cloud can stay anchored under the force of the Mistral which, for all that its critics say about it, almost always brings with it a sky of clean and polished blue.

LEFT

The wilder side of the Lubéron, devoid of swimming pools, electricity pylons, people or – except for the occasional disused mule track – roads. Members of the Resistance used to hide out in these mountains during the war, and locals who are old enough to know about such things say that there are still caches of weapons to be found in the caves and other secret corners of the upper slopes. The mountains are divided by name, and are different in atmosphere. Le Petit Lubéron, which starts just east of Cavaillon, is lower, less savage and more inhabited, with villages like Lourmarin, Vaugines and Cadenet on the south side, and Oppède, Ménerbes and Bonnieux on the north. After Bonnieux, the mountain grows into Le Grand Lubéron, the population dwindles and the views expand. From the summit, the Mourre Nègre, you can see the whole of the Vaucluse.

RIGHT

Most motorists in a hurry to get to the better-known villages of the Lubéron hardly slow down going through Robion, near Maubec. The main road is straight and undistinguished, with nothing much more than a couple of bars and a petrol station. But if you turn off and go towards the foot of the mountain, you will find the old Robion – sleepy and charming, usually watched over by two or three venerable residents perched on the stone wall by the place. All the traditional ingredients are there: a fountain with three cast-iron heads, a ring of six ancient plane trees, a bell-tower with a bell dated 1489, a church built on what remained after William of Baux destroyed the first church in 1215, and that feeling of timelessness which permeates a village where nothing much has happened for many, many years.

ABOVE

Winter in Provence is short, and often sharp. Fields turn from green to brown, and passing by them you notice that a familiar sight has disappeared. In spring and summer and autumn, from early in the morning until the sun has started to drop, it is rare to see a stretch of cultivated land without a human figure on it. He will usually be working, but you will sometimes catch him just standing, looking and ruminating. I like to think that he is taking in the beauties of nature, but I suspect he's trying to calculate the cost of fertilizer. He vanishes in the winter, and the fields, like this one near Maubec, are deserted. But he'll be back, a week or so before the rest of us realize that spring is almost here.

Maubec is a significant village in the lives of my neighbours. It is the home of the local Co-operative, and it is here that they bring their grapes to be made into Côtes du Lubéron, red and pink, and never a headache in the bottle. Wine has even seeped into the architecture. In the village, there is a wonderful doorway, framed in stone, that is like many other ancient doorways until you look at the bottom half. This has been gracefully rounded and slightly enlarged to permit the passage of a wine barrel.

The cherry orchards of the Lubéron produce thousands of tons of fruit each year, and almost as many problems for the farmer. Unlike grapes, with their grades and types and appellations, cherries are not contrôlées. They don't possess the mystique of the grape. Cherries are, well . . . cherries, almost a commodity, their individual identity lost in the vat at the jam factory. Consequently, the price per kilo is low, and the wages of picking even lower – too low, in most cases, for any self-respecting French worker. And so the farmer is obliged to look outside France for his pickers, hiring itinerant Italians or Spaniards or, with some reluctance and many reservations, gypsies. They come in caravans, and are often looked on with considerable distrust by their employer. He suspects them of disappearing one dark night with his chickens, his hunting dogs, his deeply loved twenty-year old Citroen van and God knows what else. It is an uneasy arrangement, and may partly explain why cherry-growing is declining in popularity.

You see them all over the Lubéron, tucked up against the foot of a hill, plonked in the middle of a field, or by the side of the road, one wall often painted with a fading reminder to eat Chocolat Menier or drink Suze. The stone cabanons, with their rotting wooden doors carefully locked, were once used for shelter or for the storage of farm implements. Mechanization has made them obsolete, and a pernicious little tax on any cabanon with a roof has caused many farmers to dismantle this expensive luxury and sell the roof tiles to a dealer in architectural odds and ends. I've come across many of these open-topped stone boxes, and they are invariably – unless the door has gone the way of the roof — locked.

Gordes – the Acropolis of Provence, Saint-Germain sud or whatever else it is being called nowadays – is the most photographed and, some say, the most fashionable village in the Lubéron. It is magnificently placed on a hilltop. Long and stunning views are everywhere, particularly south towards the changing colours of the Petit Lubéron. The buildings are more than well-preserved: they are immaculate. Architectural harmony is guarded by the local authorities with a zeal that extends well beyond the normal limits of planning permission. You must build, or restore, in stone. Your roof (old tiles obligatory) must have a certain pitch. Your windows cannot exceed a certain size. And yet, despite these and dozens of other expensive rules and regulations, you won't find any unoccupied ruins in Gordes. The entire village has been restored, and that well-known ally of every estate agent, the refurbisher, has departed to refurbish elsewhere. Long before the word chic was

invented, the area round the village was inhabited by neolithic man. His descendants moved up to the top of the hill in time of war, and down again in times of peace. Over the centuries, Gordes established a tradition of resistance – against the barbarians, against the beastly Baron des Adrets (who, in a fit of fury, once ordered the hanging of 17 monks) and, most recently, against the German army. In August 1944 soldiers dynamited about twenty houses and killed almost as many people in reprisal against the maquisards. After the war, the village was awarded the Croix de Guerre.

The invasions continue, but with cameras instead of guns, and Gordes in August is not the place to be if you want to get away from it all. But go anyway, in the early morning or as the sun begins to set on the village and turn it the colour of honey. You won't forget it.

The occasional pocket of cultivated land, like this one near Gordes, provides some relief from the normal strict rule of the straight line, and probably causes its owner a certain amount of irritation as he weaves his tractor in and out of the haphazardly planted trees. But inconvenience never seems to deter the Provençal farmer, and you will often come across the most inaccessible and unpromising scraps of earth that are as carefully tended as a suburban flower bed.

It started as Minerva, and then became Manancha, and now is called Ménerbes (or, if you're speaking Provençal, Menerbo). The village's first distinguished resident was St Castor, in the fourth century. Less saintly inhabitants followed, including the bandit chief Pierre de la Vache, and Karl de Rantzau, who had been implicated in the murder of the Queen of Denmark's lover.

Ménerbes, sitting on its own long, narrow hill, is perfectly placed to repel unwanted visitors. This it did in a famous fashion, earning its place in French history during the religious wars of the sixteenth century. Having chased out the Catholics in 1573, the Protestants took over as the home team, and the village became a thorn in the Papal side. Four years passed before the Catholics were ready to deal with it, but in 1577 they managed to gather a formidable anti-Ménerbes force: six Provençal regiments, a Corsican regiment, three Papal regiments, 1200 cavalry, 800 sappers and 16 cannons, a total of more than twelve thousand men

– 'An invincible Armada', one historian called it, 'against the single isolated boat of Ménerbes.'

When the attack started in September 1577, the village army was outnumbered ten to one, but it wasn't until December 1578 that Ménerbes was finally taken, and the longest siege in the history of the religious wars was over. The battle was lost, but la gloire was won.

Even today, you will hear people say that Ménerbes hasn't entirely lost the siege mentality. It has the reputation locally of being a 'closed' village, polite but distant to visitors, and less welcoming than its larger and perhaps more cosmopolitan neighbours like Gordes and Bonnieux. I don't think this is altogether true, but I do remember a man from Ménerbes describing a man from Villars as 'un estranger' – a foreigner who lived in those remote and uncharted wastes 12 miles away on the other side of the N100 road.

One of the many quarries that have bitten into the hills and mountains
of the Vaucluse to provide builders with a complete family of pierres.
There is Pierre de Ménerbes and Pierre de Lacoste – porous, friable stone
which starts the colour of cream and turns into a soft grey as the years go
by; there is Pierre de Tavel – smooth and dense, the new blocks looking
like chunks of pale toffee; there is Roche d'Espeil, hard and sand-
coloured, that comes from the high quarry between Bonnieux and
Lourmarin, with a view that could almost tempt you to take a job there.
Where other people in other places might use wood or steel or plastic,
here they use stone – for walls and floors, for tables and benches, for
sinks and baths and shelves and working surfaces. And so it's not
surprising that the best masons, the men who have a touch of the sculptor
in them, are never short of work.

A pre–bottle view of Côtes du Lubéron, the wine that has helped many
a visitor to investigate the delights of the after-lunch siesta. Some of the
best of the local wines come from venerable homes like the Château de
L'Isolette, where the Pinatel family has been in business for four
hundred years, or from the sixteenth century Château La Canorgue.
Others – Château Val-Joanis, Château La Verrerie – are more recent
arrivals, gleaming with modern equipment and producing excellent and
sometimes elegant wines that are in a different world from the Lubéron
ordinaire of twenty-five years ago.

Roussillon is not a village that hides itself modestly in the background scenery. Unlike its neighbours, it is red. Or pink. Or orange. Or rust. Or a mixture of all four, depending on the time of day and the fall of the light. It used to be the ochre capital of France, at one time producing as much as 35,000 tons a year. But why, among all the pale limestone surrounding it, did Roussillon happen to be so unusually colourful? There are two explanations. One is scholarly and geological. The other is a tale of sex, cookery, revenge and crime passionel: *the legend of Sermonde.*

She was the wife of a local lord, and she unwisely took a lover, Guillaume de Cabestan. Her husband discovered the liaison, but instead of seeking advice from a matrimonial lawyer in Avignon, he killed the lover. Not only did he kill him, but he removed his heart and used it as the basis of a râgout, *which he fed to the unsuspecting Sermonde. History doesn't tell us how she found out what she'd had for dinner, but when she did, she was so distraught that she committed suicide by throwing herself from a clifftop outside the village. Her blood stained the land around Roussillon, and thus the ochre industry was born.*

Crossing the Lubéron, you leave the rocks and ravines of the north side and come to the more gentle rolling farmland of the south. The green honeycomb and the corn-coloured lake you see here are fields in the Pays d'Aigues. This is marvellous bicycling country, less taxing on the legs and lungs than the roads on the other side of the mountain, and with no shortage of villages offering rest and refreshment to the weary. If you should find yourself in Lourmarin, for instance, you might well experience some difficulty going any further. At the last count, the village had eleven bars and restaurants. (One of them, La Fenière, has some of the best and most imaginative cooking on either side of the Lubéron).

Apt is not only the capital of the Lubéron, but also, according to a prominent notice on the outskirts of town, the world capital of fruits confits – those delicious and sugar-loaded crystallized fruits that make their annual sticky appearance each Christmas after the turkey and pudding. You will find them, along with practically everything else you could imagine eating, at the Saturday morning market, when Apt undergoes a weekly invasion. (Many have invaded in the past, including an assortment of Goths. Today's refugees from Saint-Germain and the Avenue Foch are sometimes unkindly described as the PariGoths.)

RIGHT

Springtime near Apt, when a young man's fancy turns, probably with some reluctance, to thoughts of ploughing, planting, crop-spraying and ten-hour days on the tractor. Anyone who complains about the cost of produce would perhaps think again after watching what it takes to bring something as simple as a bunch of grapes to the market. Long hours in all weathers, months of nursing and attention, the labour of picking – and always, every year, the knowledge that nature could play a dirty trick at each end of the season: spring frosts and hailstorms, or autumn monsoons. Farmers are traditionally pessimists, and they have every right to be.

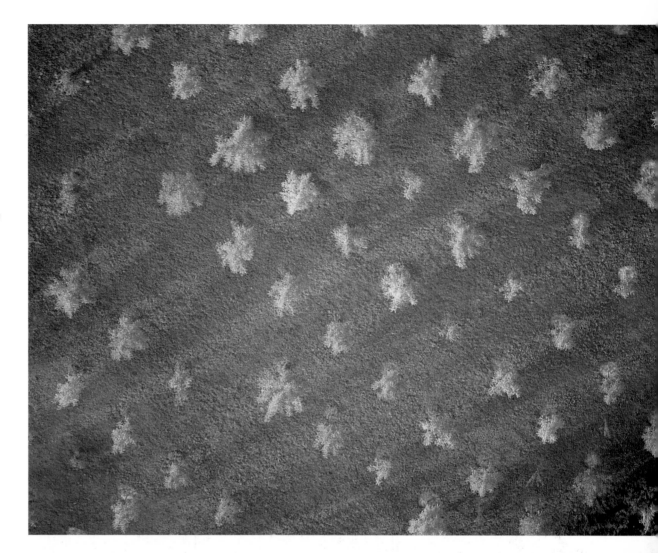

The Observatory of Haute-Provence, south of Forcalquier. From up here, it's easy to feel that there is nothing between you and the end of the world except wave afterwave of blue mountains. I have often wondered exactly what it is that one is supposed to observe from these isolated eyries: the stars at night? The storms of August? Hints of tomorrow's weather? The scientist, I'm sure, would find some high-level work to do. For the rest of us, the observatory offers the chance to listen to silence and enjoy looking at Provence from one of the best seats in the house.

The Busses dam, built across the Verdon river near Gréoux-les-Bains. The sulphurous baths of Gréoux have been renowned ever since arthritic and rheumatic Romans came to immerse themselves and soothe away the aches and pains caused by overdoing things against the Gauls. There is a modest monument, dated 126 AD, honouring thermal nymphs, and it is said that Napoleon's sister once paid the baths a visit. The site is still popular, although it lacks the magnet of a top restaurant like the one that makes Eugénie-les-Bains a four-star spa.

A rubber boat, looking rather like a modernistic flatfish, on the opaque glass surface of lake Ste-Croix. The fisherman, being a relentless optimist, is the temperamental opposite of the farmer, and is more easily pleased. He can spend the day seeing nothing, catching nothing, with never a quiver to disturb the stillness of his rod and line, and go home having had a wonderful time. Or maybe he's not really there to catch fish at all, but to escape domestic duties or a long, hot Sunday drive with his mother-in-law. I remember seeing two fishermen on the banks of the Sorgue, their rods out but their backs turned to the water, watching football on a portable television. It was a picture of utter contentment.

The enormous, dam-made lake of Ste-Croix, all the more placid and beautiful if you should come to it from the south-east, across the Grand Plan de Canjuers. This is stark country, made even less welcoming by convoys of olive-drab vehicles driven by grim-looking, almost hairless, young men who seem to be searching for World War Three. The French Army has selected this part of Provence for manoeuvres, and driving through it you cannot avoid the uncomfortable sensation that you would provide interesting diversion for a bored tank commander looking for a bit of target practice.

RIGHT

The village moored at the side of the lake. Unless you live on the coast, where they say that every window overlooking the sea is worth a million francs, water views are rare in Provence. In any case, water is not to be merely looked at; it is to be prized and guarded and used. Although Manon des Sources has long since gone, and town water has arrived, disputes between neighbours and even among families continue to trickle on over some real or imagined act of larceny that occurred three generations ago when water was diverted from its rightful place (my property) to some illegal destination (your property).

France's answer to the Grand Canyon, which is called, not very imaginatively, the Grand Canyon. It was virtually unknown until the beginning of this century, except to the locals, who claimed that it was a place where you were more than likely to bump into devils or wild and dangerous men. Then the rest of France discovered it and promoted it to a national landmark. It deserves to be – 3 miles long, in places as high (or deep) as 5000 ft and as wide as 2300 ft, it's not a spot for those who like their scenery cosy and unthreatening. One of the best views is from the Point Sublime, where there is a plaque in memory of the adventurous Monsieur Martel, whose pioneering efforts brought the canyon to public attention nearly ninety years ago.

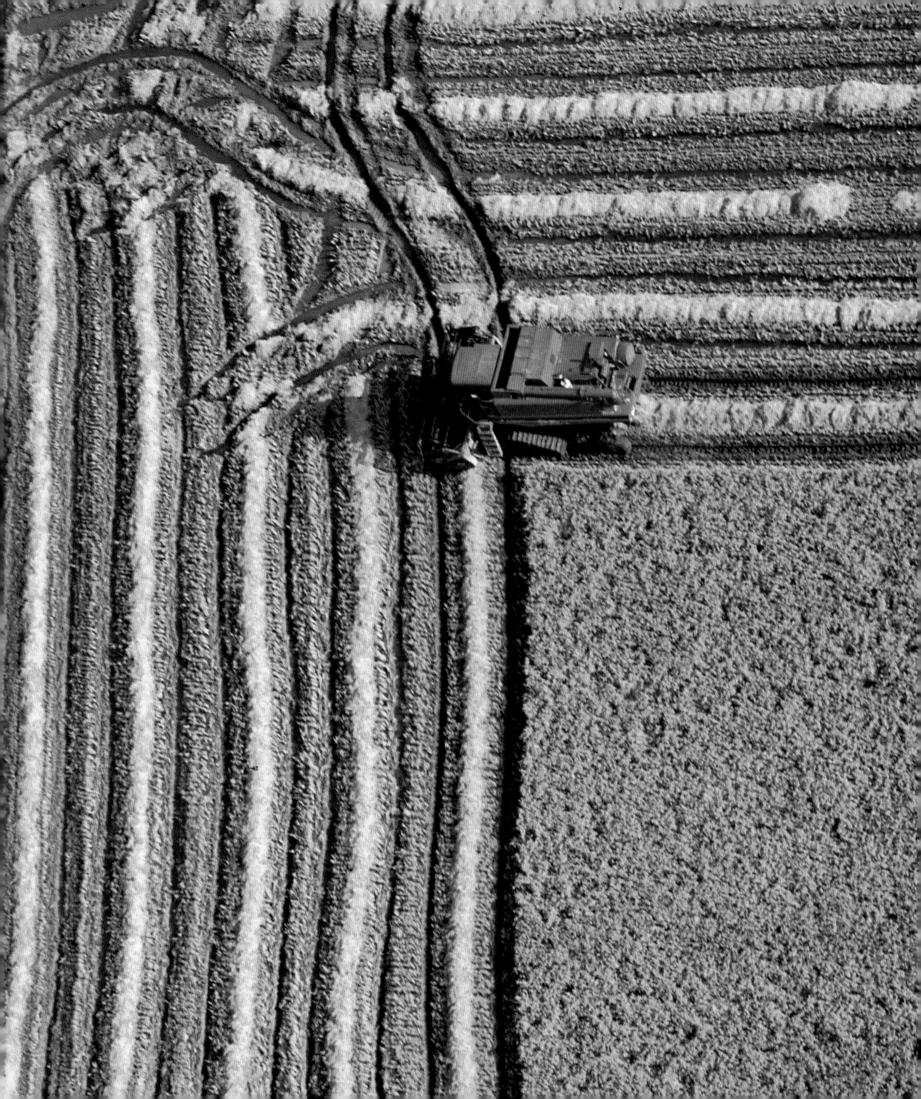

SOUTH-WEST

From the Pont du Gard to
Aigues-Mortes and the Camargue

The second most famous bridge in Provence, the Pont du Gard, was built in c. 19BC under the supervision of Agrippa, the son-in-law of Augustus. It is a monument not only to the genius of Roman engineering but also to their belief that the Roman empire would last longer than the bridge. (The design incorporates supports for scaffolding, which could be used every two thousand years or so when repairs became necessary.)

The lowest of the three arched tiers has been adapted to take a road, but if crossing by car is too tame for you, there is a more stimulating alternative: you can walk over on the narrow path that goes along the very top of the bridge. Bear in mind, however, that the drop is long enough, at 50 metres, to put an end to your sightseeing days forever if you should fall. The pathway is not protected by railings. And the Mistral has a nasty habit of blowing people off. All in all, you might prefer to take a leaf out of Pagnol's book and have a picnic overlooking the bridge.

If you're looking for the best preserved Roman temple in the world, the ancestral home of several million pairs of blue jeans, and some serious bullfighting, you'll find them all in Nîmes.

The town was developed as a colony for the veterans of Rome's conquest of Egypt (the municipal coat-of-arms, a crocodile chained to a palm tree, is a souvenir of the campaign), and, as usual, the builders and engineers were kept busy. Miles of ramparts, a 24,000-seat amphitheatre, a piped water supply and, of course, the temple, now called the Maison Carrée, which Thomas Jefferson found so impressive that he used it as the model for the Virginia State Capitol.

Nîmes later became celebrated for making and exporting textiles, and one particular line, serge de Nîmes, eventually caught the eye of a gentleman in California called Levi Strauss. The rest is history, and billions of yards of denim.

To see more elaborate outfits, you should try to be in Nîmes when the bullfighters come to town in February, Whitsun or September. There is music in the streets, the cafés operate night shifts, and the wine often flows until it's time for breakfast.

ABOVE

The Rhône froths past a sliver of an island near Aramon. One of the great natural glories of France (as any Frenchman will be happy to tell you), the Rhône is in fact a product of Switzerland. From its source in the southern Swiss Alps to its final destination in the Mediterranean is, according to the men who measure rivers, a distance of 504 miles. This, so I was told with pride by a highly nationalistic French friend, is more than twice the length of the Thames.

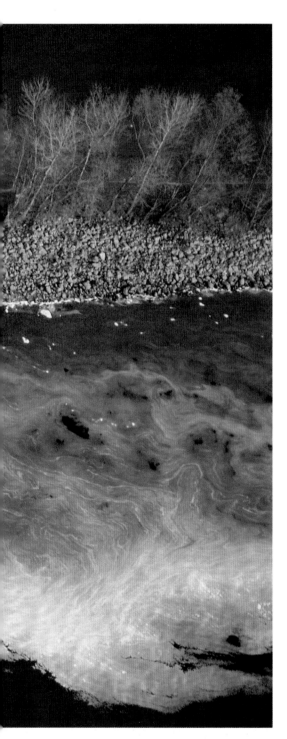

BELOW

The cemetery at Barbentane, on the slopes of the Montagnette between Avignon and Tarascon. The village market is the local mecca for aubergines, one of the world's most beautifully coloured vegetables (and the basis of a savory Provençal speciality, caviar d'aubergines). The village château, built in 1674 and lucky enough to survive the Revolution intact, is well worth taking time off from aubergine shopping to visit. You'll see furniture from the great days of the two Louis, quinze and seize, and some grandfathers among plane trees, planted in the late seventeenth century.

Field near St-Rémy in a wash of evening sunlight. For many people (including photographers), this is the best time of the day. The light is softer, the heat that scorches at noon has turned into a gentle warmth, work is over, and the cafés start to fill with men easing their backs and enjoying the cold bite of the first pastis of the evening. Eventually, they will drift home to dinner, probably closing the shutters against a spectacular sunset to watch television.

Nostradamus was born here, and Van Gogh, in one astonishingly creative year, produced about 250 paintings and drawings while he was living here. St-Rémy-de-Provence, with the baby mountains of the Alpilles as its backdrop and the remains of Roman Glanum just up the road, is a town that defies the quick visit; it pays to linger.

There is, of course, a triumphal arch, one of the first in Provence. There is one of the world's great organs in the church of St-Martin, and an organ festival each August. There are Renaissance palaces, an archaeological museum, the asylum where Van Gogh spent his year, art exhibitions and, to refresh the footsore and weary, two or three well-placed cafés on the main street which offer views of the fashionable summer residents hiding behind their sunglasses as they shop for groceries.

*Ask why people go to Arles, and
you'll get a dozen different
answers: Van Gogh, the prettiest
women in France, sausages made
from donkey meat, bullfights in
the Roman amphitheatre, one of
the liveliest Saturday markets in
Provence, the international
photographic exhibition,
museums – take your pick, and
take your time. Arles may move
slowly in the heat of summer, but
it's certainly not asleep.*

*It was once a port, and a
trading centre for sixth-century
Greek businessmen who came up
from Marseille to haggle with the
Ligurians. Later, veterans of the
Sixth Legion moved in, and
Arles grew, prospered and
celebrated its good fortune in the
monumental Roman fashion with
temples, triumphal arches, baths
and all the other necessities of the
good life. Some of these have
survived. The Arlésiennes are
still pretty. And, believe it or
not, donkey sausage is very good.*

Now high and dry, the rectangular town of Aigues-Mortes was once a port. Louis IX and a fleet of more than a thousand ships sailed from here at the start of the Seventh Crusade. But Aigues-Mortes lived up to its name, 'dead waters', the sea deserted it, and Louis' successors turned the whole place into a prison. In fact, it would be difficult to find a more naturally suitable town for locking up large numbers of people; it is enclosed by walls that are a mile long. Henry James, who travelled through Provence dropping apposite descriptions as freely as the rest of us sign our names, noted that Aigues-Mortes was like a 'billiard table without pockets'.

A thousand years ago, Provence was beginning to recover from the unwelcome attentions of the Saracens. There was time to build or restore abbeys and monasteries, and nobody was better placed to encourage that than the Provençal Saint Mayeul, whom we have to thank for countless rural churches and several abbeys. This one, Montmajour, with its stark and beautiful cloisters, set Van Gogh's imagination to work, and he wrote of knights and ladies and Provençal troubadours flitting to and fro in the moonlight. If damsels still exist, this is the kind of place you would find them.

PAGES 98 - 101

The Camargue is one of the most curious places in Provence, an exotic pocket more like a separate country than part of the mainland. The land is flat and swampy, without the customary Provençal array of vines and lavender and orchards, and the inhabitants are equally unusual. This is the résidence secondaire of thousands of pink flamingoes, taking a break from Africa, and the permanent home of white horses, bulls, a remarkable variety of aquatic birds, and, in the summer, the most determined and lethal mosquitoes in France.

And then there are the cowboys. Back in the seventeenth century, the landed gentry bought tracts of the Camargue and established ranches, where they raised cattle that could exist on the tough salt grass, and horses. The gardians came along to look after them, and you can still see their successors today, cowboy hats, leather breeches and all. (There is a theory, proudly promoted by the locals, that the first true cowboys in America, les vrais, came from the Camargue to demonstrate to the settlers of Louisiana how to deal with their beef cattle. If Louisiana had remained French, it would undoubtedly have produced the first appellation contrôlée hamburger.)

A high point of the year in the Camargue comes in May, when for two days gypsies from all over the world gather to pay their respects to Sarah, their patron saint. The town of Saintes-Maries-de-la-Mer bursts with caravans, and on 25 May the holy shrines are taken down to the sea. Other, less religious celebrations include dancing, bullfighting and the consumption of the local speciality, boeuf gardian, a stew of bull in red wine, with enough garlic to make a mosquito think twice before attacking you.

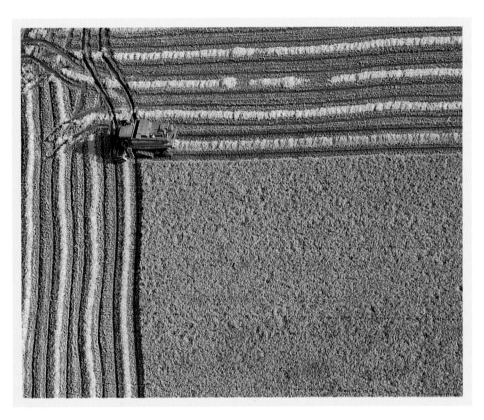

On the west bank of the Grand Rhône. The river divides the Camargue
of the cowboys from the eastern part of the Camargue, which only an
industrialist could love. In the east you will find places like Fos, where
factories roam the range, and seldom is heard a discouraging word above
the grumbling of heavy machinery.

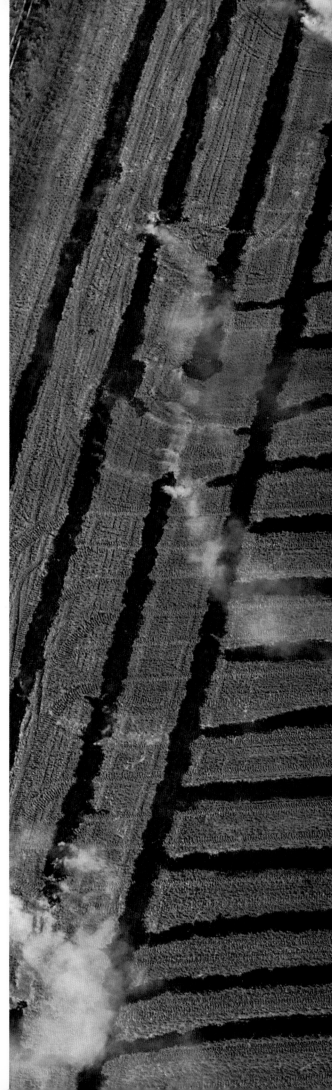

The Camargue's big crop is salt. Monks spotted it in the Middle Ages, and modern methods have taken over where they left off. Nearly half of all the salt in France is collected from the giant pans like these, near Port-St-Louis. It is, as you might expect, a nonpareil among salts, a salt for kings and presidents and writers of cookbooks – large, crunchy crystals which are the perfect accompaniment for fresh radishes. The best of the best, which are known as les fleurs du sel, are good enough to eat just sprinkled on bread, and unforgettable when eaten with fresh truffles.

Neatness and order, so apparent on land, extends into the sea at the Golfe de Fos, where tidy-minded fishermen seem to have arranged their nets specifically for the photograph. The waters round here and east towards Marseille are breeding grounds for the small army of fish that end their days as bouillabaisse – that pungent, saffron-flavoured cross between a soup and a stew that is best eaten with the sleeves rolled up and a bib around the neck. All along the coast, you are likely to hear vigorous arguments about where to find the best bouillabaisse (Toulon and Marseille are the front runners), and exactly what should go in it. The Toulonnais add potatoes, which purists in Marseille regard as heresy. The one thing everyone agrees on is that bouillabaisse doesn't travel. You need Mediterranean fish on your dorstep, or it's not the real thing.

105

South-East

*From Aix-en-Provence
and Marseilles to Nice*

Lambesc is a calm and pretty oasis just off the road made famous in song and accident statistics, the Nationale Sept. Before the construction of the autoroutes, the N7 was the main highway to the joys of the Côte d'Azur, and motorists consumed by holiday fever would perform miracles of recklessness to reach the beach 15 minutes before the car in front of them. This had its inevitable tragic results, and still does. Of all the roads in Provence, the N7 demands the most concentration, and a healthy measure of cowardice when faced with an oncoming and almost airborne Peugeot 205 playing leapfrog with slow traffic.

Market day in the village of Rognes, south of the Lubéron. In spite of the inexorable spread of supermarkets (they now supply more than 50 per cent of all the food bought in France), the small market is far from dead, and as long as people prefer charm over plastic-wrapped efficiency it will continue to survive. Market shopping is

addictive - convivial, unhurried, pleasantly noisy. You can browse, buy a single peach and watch the formidable French housewife peering with quite unnecessary suspicion at a tray of identically plump tomatoes before indicating, with an imperious finger, which will be fresh enough for her evening salad.

109

The straightforward appearance of these vines north of Aix shows no sign of the complications that are now inescapable if you should have any ambitions of becoming a vigneron. *An essential part of every vineyard, in addition to good French soil, is a bureaucratic mulch of paperwork – applications, attestations and detailed descriptions, followed, if you're lucky, by approvals and permissions. You want to rip out some tired old Syrah vines and replace them with Cabernet-Sauvignon? The government must be advised. Forms must be completed. Exact numbers must be specified, and an inspector will come to ensure that you haven't slipped in an extra row. It's enough to drive a man to drink.*

PAGES 111-113

There is something insidious about Aix. You go there filled with worthy intentions – the Tapestry Museum, the cathedral, the palaces and churches – but it requires a considerable effort of will to stick to your programme. Aix tends to distract you with its charm, with its cafés, with its fascinating flow of humanity, with the seductive midday scents of lunch, and it is only the disciplined seeker after knowledge who can ignore these in favour of a visit to the dinosaur eggs in the Museum of Natural History.

If you are one of these admirable people, you will have a busy and absorbing time. Aix began with the Romans, became the capital of the Counts of Provence in the thirteenth century, established its university in 1409 and enjoyed the rule of the good king René (a well-loved figure in Aix, partly because he introduced popular fêtes to the town, and the Muscat grape to Provence). Later, as the centre of regional government in the seventeenth and eighteenth centuries, Aix was the home of wealthy magistrates who built themselves suitably splendid houses.

And so history has left its mark, mostly elegant and always interesting, and you could spend weeks in Aix without feeling culturally deprived. But man must eat, and there is no better place to do that than the terrace of the Deux Garçons on a sunny day. (Historical note: the décor dates from the Empire period, and the waiters are ageless.)

To the east of Aix, and looking more prominent than ever
after the forest fire which scalded its slopes, Montagne
Sainte-Victoire presides over what is now known as
Cézanne country. The mountain obsessed him, and it
appears in his paintings more than sixty times. During his
lifetime, which was spent almost entirely in Aix, Cézanne
was not the revered figure he is today. Aix sneered at his
work, and eventually the artist bit back. To anyone asking
to see his latest canvases, his response was short and
discouraging. 'I shit on you', he would say. There's no
answer to that.

The coastline near Carry-le-Rouet, a town that has the
distinction of staging a strange and possibly unique event.
Each February, if you're drawn to such oddities, you can go
and participate in the Great Annual Sea-Urchin Festival,
and pay homage to the spiky delicacy before eating it. The
only other gastronomic spectacle I know that rivalled this for
curiosity value was the attempt a few years ago by the
villagers of Bedoin to enter the Guinness Book of Records
with the world's largest omelette — a masterpiece of a
thousand eggs which was whisked to perfection in
cement–mixers.

PAGES 116-125

Marseille is the oldest city in France, one of the world's top ten ports, bastion of bouillabaisse and pastis, stamping ground of Le Pen, home sweet home for the French mafia and first stop for thousands of immigrants from Europe and North Africa. It also has its own olive oil-based soap and has appropriated the national anthem. (Although, in fact, La Marseillaise was composed in Strasbourg.) Say what you may about Marseille, but it is not dull.

It all began in 600 BC, when a Greek expedition came and saw and settled, calling their new discovery Massalia. It prospered from the start, and by the second century BC, the city had a population of 50,000, protected by a beneficial alliance with Rome. The city elders then made their big mistake. They changed sides, threw in their lot with Pompey, and unwisely provoked the displeasure of Caesar, who continued his winning streak by seizing the city.

The centuries passed, Rome declined and fell, and Marseille found itself under attack from all the marauders of the day – Goths, Franks, Saracens; any group of plunderers with an army and an acquisitive disposition couldn't resist the idea of having a port to call their own. It

wasn't until the eleventh century, when the Crusaders needed a convenient departure point for the Holy Land, that Marseille's fortunes improved.

Up and down they went over the next few hundred years, going through sieges, a long and disastrous quarrel with Louis XIV, a plague epidemic, the upheavals of the Revolution and squabbles with Napoleon. But Marseille survived to boom again when the Suez Canal opened in 1869, and has continued ever since to be an important presence in France, although not greatly loved by the central government in Paris (a sentiment that is reciprocated by the Marseillais).

Marseille's reputation is blotchy, or worse. The recent ambulance wars didn't help; nor did The French Connection. But the idea that a visit to the city is a risk to life and limb has been exaggerated. Like New York, there are places to tread carefully, places not to tread at all, and places where the worst that can happen to you is failing to catch the eye of an overworked waiter, such as the Vieux Port, which is a fine spot to start and end a day in Marseille.

In the morning, you can have a café breakfast and

wander over to the fish market on the Quai des Belges. Fresh fish by the ton, and a constant babble of salesmanship, insult and tall stories from the gentlemen with scaly hands and rubber aprons. And in the evening, you'll have a grandstand view of the sunset.

Whatever else you do during the day, you should take the short ferry ride from the Quai des Belges to the most picturesque jail outside San Francisco, the Château d'If. Prisoners are now kept elsewhere, but some of the cells have been personalized with the names of previous occupants, either real (Mirabeau) or imaginary (Dumas's Count of Monte Cristo). A consolation for captives, and a delight for the visitor, is the view of the city rising from the sea.

Back on dry land, there is a grand muddle of architectural styles – Gothic-Renaissance, neo-Byzantine, Napoleonic, Art Deco – alleys and boulevards, seedy bars and pompous palaces, the end result (so far, at least) of 2600 years of human habitation. You won't be bored.

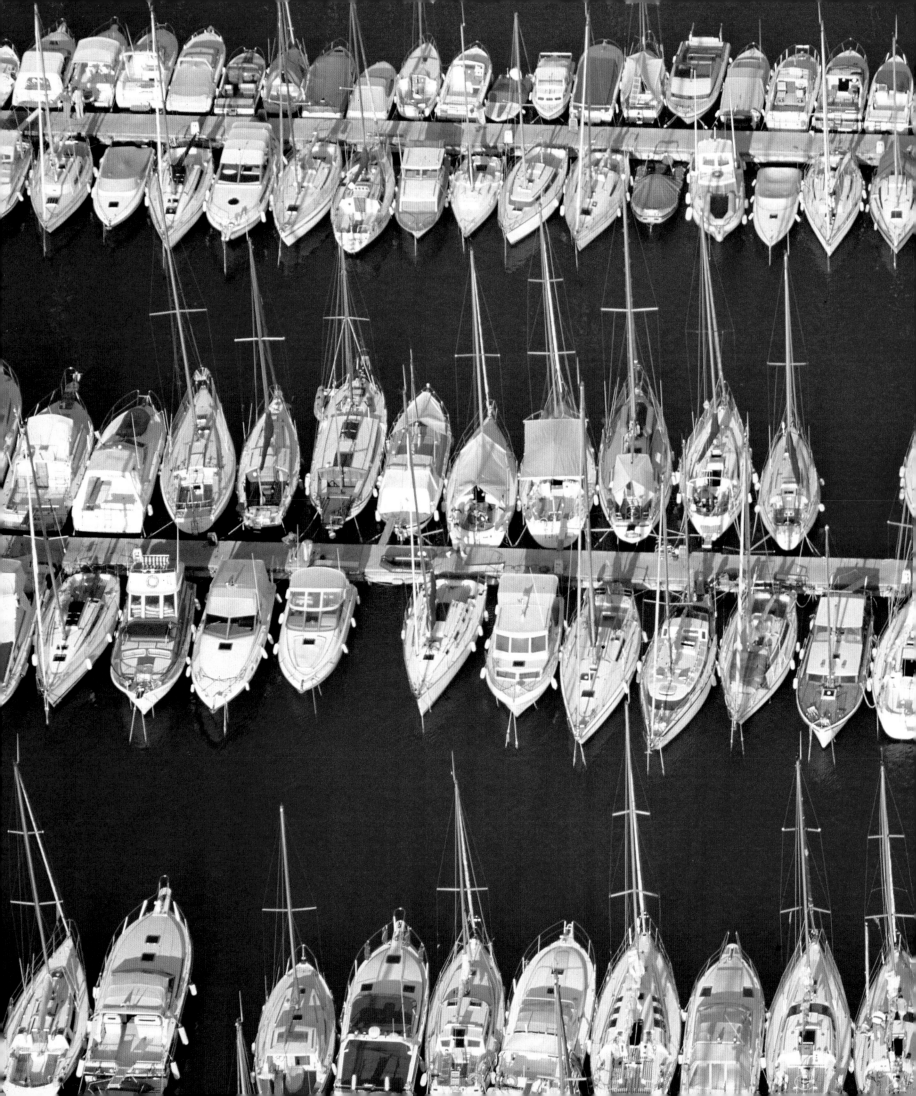

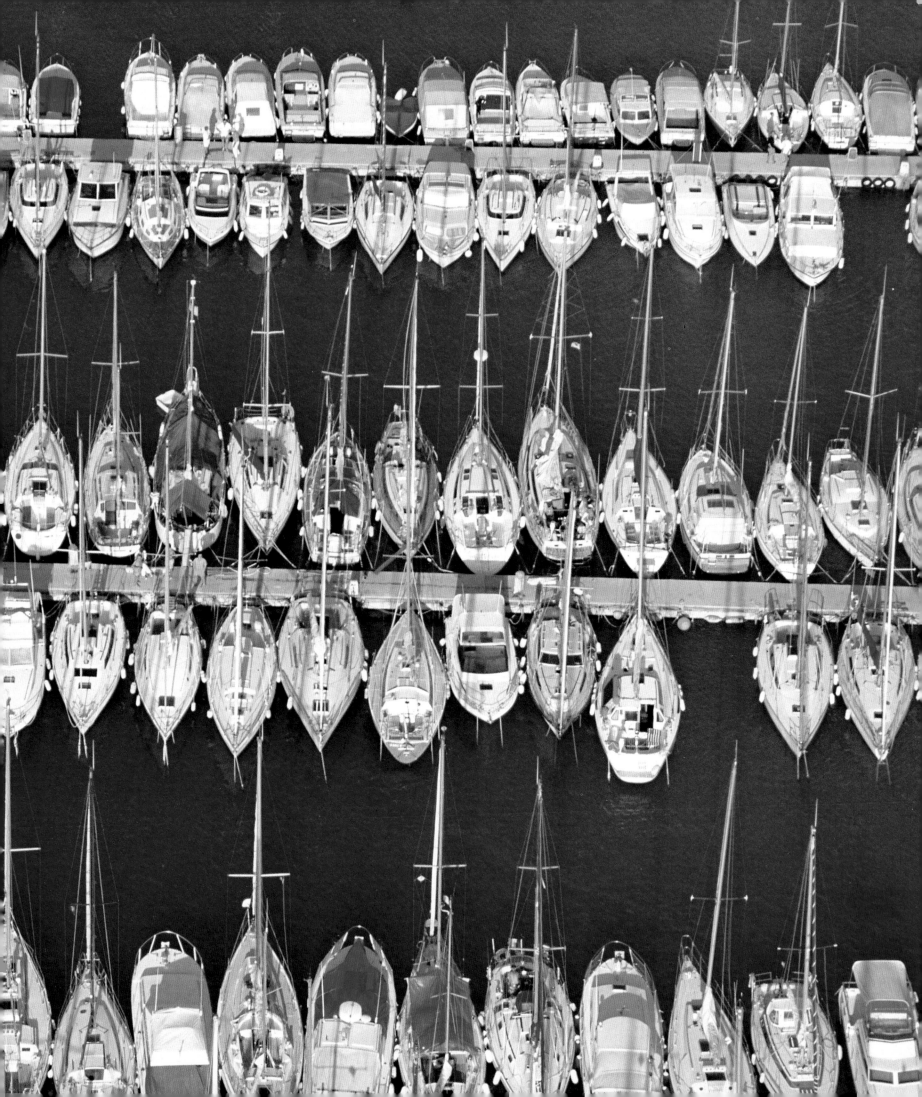

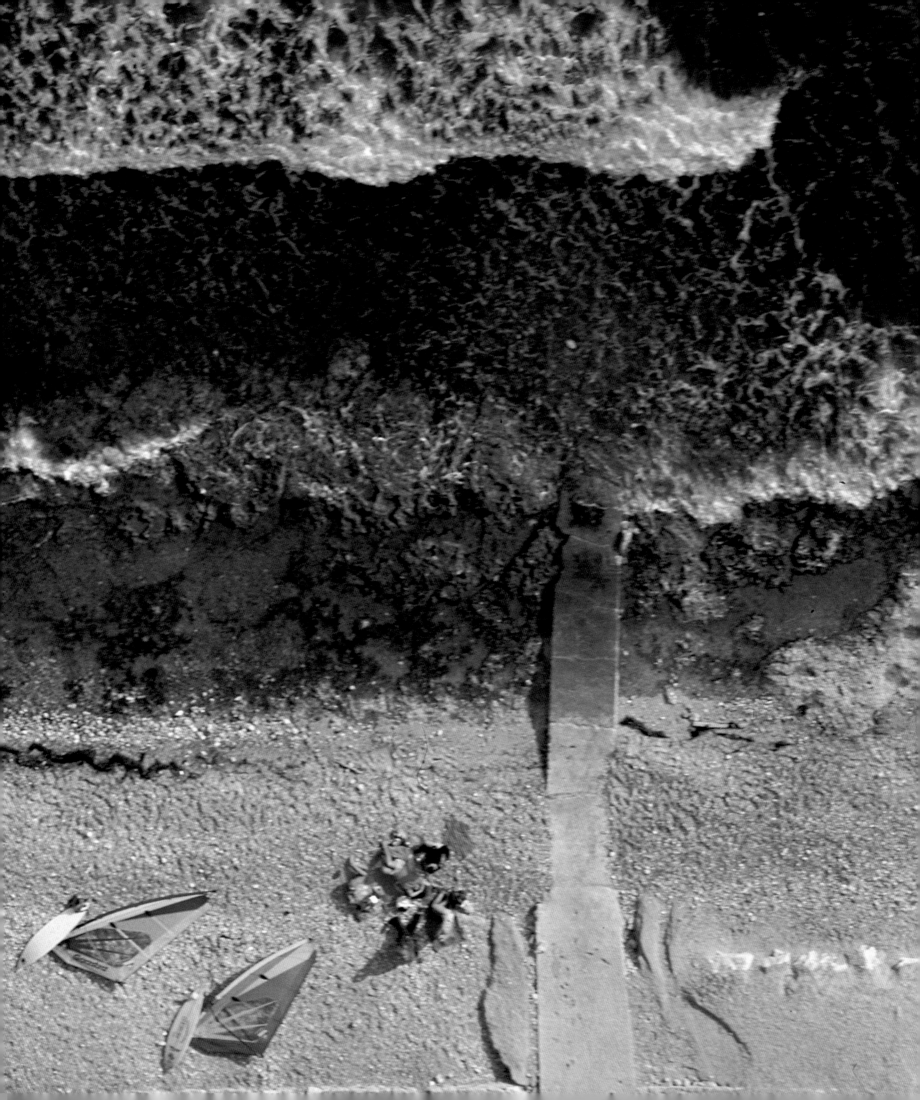

If you leave the Chemin du Roucas Blanc, and climb the hill until your legs ache, you'll arrive at the basilica of Notre-Dame de la Garde. When you get your breath back, you'll be able to appreciate the great spread of Marseille. The only better view of the city is enjoyed by the giant gold Madonna, ten metres tall, who gazes out from her ornate pedestal on the roof.

LEFT

Domed and striped and in no danger of falling down (more than 400 marble columns are under the roof to take the weight), the Cathédrale de la Major *sits in the sun behind Marseille harbour. This is Le Panier, the oldest district in an old city where, not far from the cathedral, you'll find Puget's Vieille-Charité, a seventeenth-century hospice originally built as a shelter for the homeless, which would put many palaces to shame. Today, it is home for art and photography exhibitions, and the museum of Mediterranean Archaeology.*

ABOVE

There is an image of the Mediterranean coastline that is perpetuated each year by articles telling us that there is not a yard of unpolluted, uninhabited space between Menton and the Camargue. It is all taken up, so they insist, by sunbathers (clad, topless or nude), water-ski concessions, expensive fish restaurants, yacht marinas and beach vendors hoping to sell you plastic watches or suspiciously cheap jewellery. There is a lot of truth in this, but there are some beautiful exceptions. This is one of them, less than ten miles from the centre of Marseille, just east of Cap Croisette. Alas, you need a boat to enjoy it.

LEFT & ABOVE

Certain aspects of progress, while they may be impressive in terms of technological achievement, should have been sunk at birth. The jet ski is one of them. The noise grates on human ears, and probably deafens fish, and the fuel residue left on the surface turns a swim into an evil–tasting horror. Here you see a jet ski thudding over the waves off Cap Morgiou. Later – same day, same place – we saw a cleaner, more tranquil method of moving across water.

Between Marseille and Cassis, the coastline has been nibbled away by the sea to form a series of small, rocky inlets – quiet, secluded and clean. These are the Calanques, and if you're lucky enough to have a boat, or a friend with a boat, you can leave crowded beaches and restaurants behind you and treat yourself to one of the great pleasures of summer, the pique-nique nautique. *For once, the food is much less important than the setting. Dress is optional. The Mediterranean is your wine cooler, and you can refresh yourself between courses by slipping over the side, glass in hand, while the finishing touches are being applied to the cheese board. There are worse ways of spending a hot day.*

LEFT

The Calanques form a series of natural breakwaters along the coast between Marseille and Cassis. Many of them can only be reached by sea, but the resourceful pedestrian can find the occasional footpath which ends in a fine froth of limestone against the limestone.

LEFT, ABOVE & OVERLEAF

Cassis, so everyone says, is reminiscent of Saint-Tropez before the chic and the famous moved in. There is one big difference, though: cars are not allowed in the central area round the port, so the sounds you hear by the sea in Cassis are more likely to be the snap of sails and the rattle of rigging than the rumble of overheated engines.

The port is tucked in between limestone hills to the west, and the great bulk of Cap Canaille to the east, and is almost too pretty to be true. White cliffs, beaches, narrow streets, waterfront restaurants (one of them specializes in a superlative ratatouille which has the consistency of thick jam) – Cassis has all this, and its own dry white wine, which is good enough to have held appellation status for nearly sixty years. For an introductory nip, you can go to the old caves of Clos Sainte-Madeleine. Very few people leave without buying a bottle or two.

Sleepy Brignoles, renowned for its prunes, is not on the visiting list of most tourists, but any true student of the bizarre should make a point of going there to spend a few hours marvelling at the frequently eccentric contents of the Musée du Pays Brignolais. There are, as you would expect, several items to excite the antiquarian's interest, notably 'La Gayole', an early (second- or third-century) Christian sarcophagus. But other treasures are less frequently found in more conventional museums. For example: a concrete canoe, a wooden model of Milan Cathedral, a stuffed weasel, and a charming depiction of a lady in a boat accompanied by a pig smoking a cigar.

Follow the road in the foreground, and you'll end up nudging bumpers in Cannes with thousands of other motorists. But turn off to the south, head for the hills, and you'll find yourself in the quiet green forests of the Massif des Maures. This is chestnut and cork tree country. Bamboo also grows here, and a bush whose dense sturdy roots are used to make the pipes of Cogolin. Chestnut lovers should make a short, sweet stop at Collobrières for a fix of marrons glacés *and a look at what is reputed to be the largest chestnut tree in Provence, with a girth of more than thirty feet.*

LEFT

The empty leafy sea around La Garde-Freinet, a village that was home to the Saracens a thousand years ago. They are chiefly remembered for their pillaging of the surrounding countryside, but in quieter moments between raids, they also taught the locals all about cork – how to strip it from the trees, season it and carve it into those invaluable plugs for wine bottles. In the nineteenth century, this was La Garde-Freinet's village industry, and the forest you see here would have been alive with corkers. Now, if you see anybody, it's likely to be an intrepid hiker or a French family looking for a suitably sauvage spot for a picnic.

ABOVE

Wind ruffling the treetops of an orchard near Les Arcs, a village which, although small, has something to offer both the historian in us and the beast that needs to be fed. The church has a sixteenth-century fresco depicting the miracle of Saint Rosseline and, for some reason that is not immediately obvious, an ancient mechanical crib. The stomach is served at Le Logis du Guetteur, a restored castle with a pool and a good restaurant. It's a very pleasant stop, not far from the autoroute, where you can pause to brace yourself for the final Grand Prix dash to the coast.

Looking like green mushrooms on stilts, parasol pines are as evocative of the south as pink wine and wild thyme. They even have their own signs on the autoroutes, and when you see them you know that you've left the harsher countryside of northern Provence behind. A stroll in a parasol pine forest, like this one north of Fréjus, is a wonderfully gentle contrast to slogging up and down limestone crags. It is soft and silent underfoot, with a thick cushion of fallen needles that muffles the sound of your footsteps, and the air is cool and clean and faintly aromatic. And the trees themselves, although often twisted by the wind, somehow always manage to look graceful.

St-Tropez has an August reputation: too many people, too much traffic, overbooked hotels and overpriced restaurants. It is sometimes called Montparnasse-sur-mer, in recognition of the bands of café refugees from Paris. But go in April or May, and it's a very different place. Without the crowds, the charm is visible, and you can see why it attracted artists at the beginning of the century and Mademoiselle Bardot later on. At the tail-end of the season (last week in September and first week in October), when le tout Paris has gone home, the town celebrates with the Nioulargue, an annual race between some of the most handsome yachts afloat. And in winter – which can be surprisingly cold, as St-Tropez faces north – there is a pleasant, lazy atmosphere of a community enjoying virtual hibernation.

Les Adrets, in the Esterel, where brigands used to pounce on innocent tourists and relieve them of their cash (a practice which, some critics say, still continues on the coast). The village roofs, with one or two bright exceptions, are clad in the curved and mellow tiles that are supposed to follow the contours of a woman's thigh. It has been many years since tiles were moulded in this painstaking fashion, and a revival of the art is unlikely. Modern, diet-conscious Provençal ladies don't have the necessary breadth of thigh.

The horseshoe-shaped bay of Agay, with the hills of the Esterel in the background. Collectors of panoramic views will find plenty to take their breath away (literally, if they go on foot) on top of the Pic de l'Ours, the Pic du Cap Roux or Mont Vinaigre, 2000 ft high and worth every step.

Cannes first became fashionable thanks to an outbreak of cholera. In 1834, Lord Brougham was on his way to Italy when his stately progress was blocked by a cordon sanitaire, *which closed the border and obliged his lordship to break his journey in the one and only hotel that Cannes possessed. He found the little fishing village much to his liking, bought some land and built a house. Other bigwigs followed, and the fishermen soon found themselves rubbing shoulders with the English aristocracy, as well as the Tsar of Russia's family and entourage. Cannes had arrived on the social map, and has stayed there ever since.*

The aristocracy today is more likely to come from Hollywood than the House of Lords, and you will see the barons of Beverly Hills each year at the Film Festival, toying with their loups de mer *and cellular phones. It's an unreal place, Cannes, frenzied in the summer, flat in the winter, and breathtakingly expensive all year long.*

Antibes has undergone a distinct personality change since it was a stern fortified town on the old Provence/Savoy border. It was here that Scott and Zelda Fitzgerald discovered the pleasures of the South of France, and made their reputation as party champions of the 1920s. Picasso spent some time here too, and his stay is commemorated by a fine collection of his work in the Musée Picasso. The rich park their boats in the harbour before dropping in on their equally rich friends in the manicured glades of Cap d'Antibes, leaving the rest of us to mill around in the morning market and watch helicopters coming and going from the decks of liner-sized yachts.

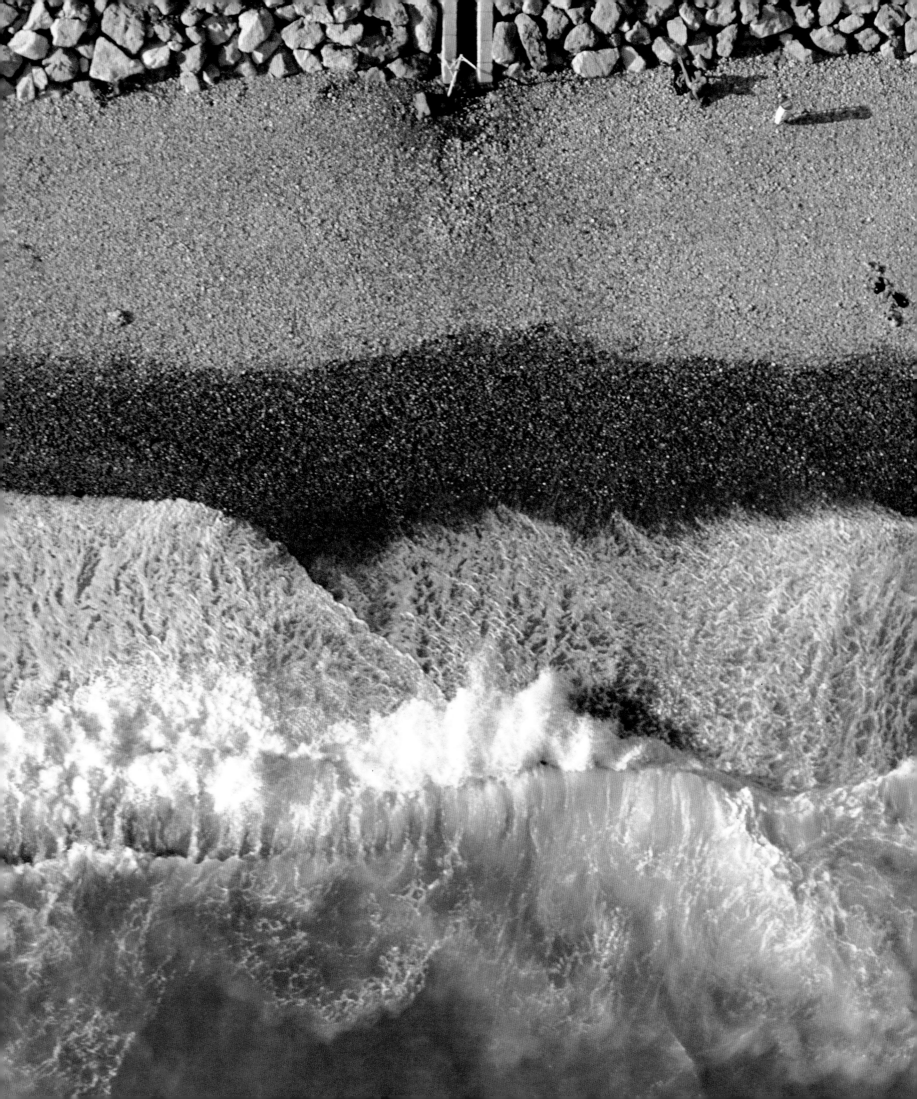

PAGES 154–159

Unlike Cannes, its neighbour just down the coast, Nice has a life of its own outside festivals, conventions and tourists. These come to town, certainly, but their departure doesn't seem to make any difference. Nice continues to go about its business throughout the year, and it is one of the most pleasant places you could hope to stay over a winter weekend.

The niçois food alone is well worth the trip – a mixture of French and Italian, served in hundreds of restaurants that vary from hole–in–the–wall bistros to grand establishments like the Négresco or Maximin's converted casino. In between meals, you can take your pick of museums – modern art, naive art, Beaux Arts, Chagall, Matisse, archaeological relics, Napoleonic odds and ends – or just wander through the streets of Vieux Nice to the flower market in the Cours Saleya.

There is baroque architecture, there are a thousand cafés, there is Alziari for some of the best olive oil in Provence, and Auer for celestial chocolates and jams, there is the long and elegant sweep of the Promenade des Anglais – there is, in fact, far too much to see and do in a mere weekend. Why not take a week?

INDEX